SIGHT SINGING

Pitch · Interval · Rhythm

SIGHT SINGING

Pitch · Interval · Rhythm

Samuel Adler

EASTMAN SCHOOL OF MUSIC

W · W · NORTON & COMPANY

NEW YORK

Copyright © 1979 by W. W. Norton & Company, Inc.
Published simultaneously in Canada by George J. McLeod Limited, Toronto. Printed in the United States of America.
All Rights Reserved

FIRST EDITION

Library of Congress Cataloging in Publication Data
Adler, Samuel, 1928–
  Sight singing.
  1. Sight-singing.
MT870.A243   784.9'4   78–10772
ISBN 0–393–95052–2

1 2 3 4 5 6 7 8 9 0

Contents

PART TWO Rhythmic Studies

Preface

Aims of This Book

We are living in a time when the technical demands on musicians are increasing with every passing year. There are at least two major reasons for this continuing phenomenon. First, the repertoire we are expected to perform not only grows larger and more difficult with each newly composed score, but also embraces music from historical periods dating back to medieval times. Only thirty or forty years ago, most concerts presented music from the time of J. S. Bach to the early twentieth century, with the greatest emphasis on the years between 1750 and 1880; this is no longer true. Second, the fluctuating or unstable use of tonality, which is commonplace in contemporary music, places an additional burden on our ear and our sense of pitch relationship. From the nineteenth century on, the extent of tonality and stress on the tonal center has varied from composer to composer and sometimes even from work to work in one composer's oeuvre. As a direct result of the broadening of our repertoire, we observe in works from as long ago as the twelfth century that ideas of tonality and modality were handled in ways seemingly totally unrelated to our musical thinking today.

With the areas of specialization open to musicians becoming more diversified, it becomes essential to take a hard look at the ways in which the performing, composing, conducting, or scholarly musician is preparing for the conditions that exist in the profession today. The major concern of this book is musical literacy. It has always seemed to me that the ability to read music, regardless of style, period, or complexity, is the most essential tool for the professional musician. Yet much of the literature dealing with this crucial area of reading, hearing, and perception is inadequate to meet the new demands placed on the music student. Most texts concentrate on melodic, harmonic, and rhythmic exercises which reflect the narrow, though magnificent, period of creativity from 1750 to 1880. In this volume, I have focused on the one musical element common to all styles and creative periods, namely the interval. I contend that if you sing by intervals at all times, you will be able to read music that is tonal, modal, pantonal, nontonal, or a combination of all of these means of organization and polarization. The other area of concentration is rhythm. The student will be drilled in basic rhythmic problems, at the same time encountering the more complex rhythmic configurations found so frequently in the works of the past twenty-five years. It is hoped that a greater awareness of the entire scope of music will result from this procedure. For reasons of immediacy and practicality, I have chosen to present a multitude of exercises rather than abundance of text.

How to Use This Book

It is suggested that the student practice for about fifteen minutes a day to master the melodic as well as the rhythmic exercises. The book is structured for use in a four-semester musicianship course, but it may also serve for individualized instruction of anyone wishing to improve his sight singing, dictation, or rhythmic skills. Furthermore, it could function as an introduction to any conducting class in order to heighten the students' awareness of pitch and rhythm. Finally, the exercises could be used for warmup by choral groups to strengthen their ability to cope with intervallic and rhythmic problems.

The specific method of singing is left up to the instructor or the student. A solfège system may certainly be used. In that case, I would strongly recommend the use of the stationary *do*, since no key relationships are espoused anywhere in the book. Alternatively, a system of numbers may be utilized, labeling each note from C to B chromatically. The syllable *la* or *ta* or *lu* may be used in singing the exercises. I have never been too concerned about the exact method of singing a melody or the quality of tone produced in a sight singing class as long as the pitches and the rhythms are correct. A neutral syllable, such as *ta, la, da, du,* etc., should be employed in the performance of the rhythmic exercises in Part Two. Humming must be discouraged because it obscures articulation of melody as well as rhythm.

It is of primary importance that the first (melodic) and second (rhythmic) parts of the book be used simultaneously or concurrently. The reason they are presented separately is because the rhythmic portion does not require the same amount of time as the melodic chapters. Therefore, it should be rather simple to complete Chapters X, XI, and XII by the time the student has reached the last section of Chapter III and is ready to tackle the rhythmic exercises presented there. If the material in the rhythm chapters has not been mastered, the exercises based on nonrhythmic fragments should be postponed until such time as the student has a good command of the rhythmic techniques contained in the first three chapters of Part Two.

Still another imaginative way of utilizing this text: every week or so, the student should be assigned a nonrhythmic exercise from Part One and asked to "rhythmitize" it. Similarly, a rhythmic exercise from Part Two should be "melodized" with pitches from the nonrhythmic exercise in Part One that is being drilled at that time. These creative exercises should be performed in class by the "composer," sight-read by the group, or given as dictation in rhythmic and melodic drills. It is also urged that extensive use be made of each student's particular instrument, for too often dictation drills are confined to the piano. This technique has many advantages: it provides an excellent opportunity to utilize the instrumental and vocal resources of the class; it "equalizes" the position of the nonpianist; and it provides the exercises with a greater variety of tonal color. Duets may be used frequently during the course of study and a typical assignment may read, for example:

1. Melodize Duet No. "X" using only major or minor seconds in the upper part and only major or minor thirds in the lower part.

2. Take a rhythmic exercise in Chapter XI and melodize it, using a Phrygian or other modal scale.

3. Take a nonrhythmic melodic fragment from Chapter V and rhythmitize it with the rhythmic pattern of Exercise "Y" in Chapter XII.

4. Take a series of chords in Chapter VIII and set them rhythmically to Exercise "Z" in Chapter XIV.

As has already been mentioned, all these exercises should be sight-read in class and performed on a variety of instruments.

Canons have been provided to afford the student the greatest amount of practice in "holding his own" in simple polyphony while he enjoys singing rounds. It would be most desirable if the class would perform the canons a cappella after an initial period of instrumental support and help. Of course, if instruments are available, they should also be used in the performance of the rounds, so that the first and third entrances, for example, may be vocal while the second and fourth could be played by instruments.

Conclusion

It is my sincere hope that this modest volume will help strengthen musical literacy in its application to all kinds of music, regardless of style or tonal organization. Further, I hope it will facilitate the instruction of this most crucial subject at a time when music making, in all its manifestations, is proliferating wildly and multiplicity of musical styles and techniques has become a permanent reality.

Samuel Adler

Acknowledgments

I am greatly indebted to a number of people for their aid and encouragement in the writing, testing, and final completion of this book. First I'd like to mention Jan DeGaetani, who inspired the initial idea for this system of sight singing by describing the difficulties students experienced in her master classes when asked to perform unorthodox intervallic combinations. Further, I'd like to express my appreciation to the Theory Department of the Eastman School of Music, particularly to Dorothy Payne (now at the University of Texas in Austin), William Penn, David Beach, and Robert Gauldin, as well as to Jerold Graue, chairman of the Department of Musicology here, for their constructive criticism and for the opportunities they provided to test much of the material. To my secretary, Wende Persons, goes special thanks for her untiring devotion in the preparation of the manuscript. Last but certainly not least, I'd like to express my special gratitude to Claire Brook, music editor of W. W. Norton, for the splendid editing of the manuscript, and for being so very supportive in all aspects leading to the completion of the project.

PART ONE

Melodic Studies

CHAPTER I

Preliminaries

Two prerequisites will facilitate our study of singing by interval before we begin:

1. Instant recognition of all pitches on, above, and below the staff in both the treble and the bass clefs. After the first few chapters we shall discuss and practice exercises in the alto and tenor clefs as well.

2. A thorough knowledge of all major and minor scales would certainly help, even though, as will be emphasized throughout this book, not all the exercises are based on our "common practice" tonal system. Nevertheless, the terms *major* and *minor* occur so frequently in the designation of intervals that a brief time should be spent to review key signatures as well as the half step–whole step construction of our major and minor scales. Modal scales and synthetic scales will be discussed and analyzed later on in the text.

Major and Minor Scales

The Relationships of Keys in the Circle of Fifths

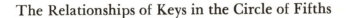

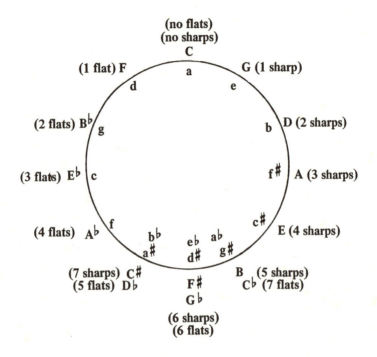

(no flats)
(no sharps)
C

(1 flat) F   a   G (1 sharp)

d   e

(2 flats) B♭   b   D (2 sharps)
g

(3 flats) E♭   c   f♯   A (3 sharps)

c♯
(4 flats) A♭   f   E (4 sharps)
b♭   e♭ a♭
a♯   d♯ g♯

(7 sharps) C♯   B (5 sharps)
(5 flats) D♭   F♯   C♭ (7 flats)
G♭

(6 sharps)
(6 flats)

Major Scales and Their Relative Minors

The major scale is constructed in the following manner: *

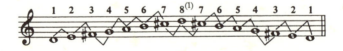

There are three types of minor scale.

1. Simple, modal, natural, or pure minor:

* Brackets above the notes signify whole steps and those below, half steps.

2. Melodic minor:

The melodic minor ascends with the sixth and seventh degrees raised and then lowered again when descending. The descending melodic minor is like the simple minor scale. Occasionally, you will find the ascending form of the melodic minor scale used in the downward direction. These instances are rare.

3. Harmonic minor:

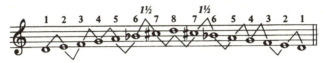

This scale is the same as the simple minor, except that the seventh degree is raised both ascending and descending.

Relationship between Major and Minor Scales

Each major scale has a relative minor. The key signature is the same, but that is the extent of the relationship. To find the relative minor scale, count down three half steps (a minor third) from the key (tonic) note:

C major related to A minor (no sharps or flats in the signature).
D major related to B minor (both have two sharps in the signature).

Conversely, to find the relative major of a minor scale, count up three half steps (a minor third) from the key (tonic) note:

F minor related to A♭ major (both have four flats in the signature).
E minor related to G major (both have one sharp in the signature).
Here is the full table:

Exercises

I. Write out the following scales by half and whole steps, without signature.

Example

b minor melodic

1. D minor, melodic	11. A minor, melodic
2. E♭ major	12. E♭ minor, harmonic
3. F minor, harmonic	13. G minor, simple
4. A major	14. G major
5. C♯ major	15. D♭ major
6. C♯ minor, simple	16. E major
7. F♯ major	17. F♯ minor, melodic
8. C minor, harmonic	18. B♭ minor, harmonic
9. D major	19. B♭ major
10. A♭ major	20. C♭ major

II. Write out the key signatures for the twenty scales above in both the treble clef and the bass clef.

Example

b minor melodic

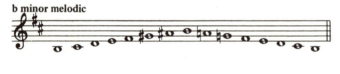

b minor melodic

CHAPTER II

Learning about Intervals

Simple and Compound Intervals

An interval is the distance between pitches (in other words, the difference or space between two tones). Intervals can be divided into two major groups:

1. *Simple intervals:* those which are smaller than an octave, or within the chromatic scale of an octave (C–C′).
2. *Compound intervals:* those which are larger than an octave.

Examples of simple intervals:

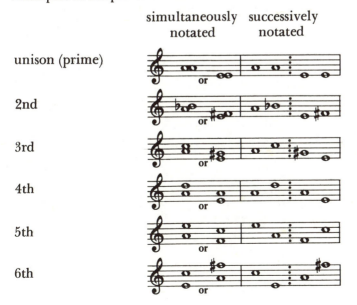

	simultaneously notated	successively notated
unison (prime)		
2nd		
3rd		
4th		
5th		
6th		

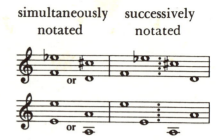

7th

8ve

The compound intervals are:

9th (compound 2nd)

10th (compound 3rd)

11th (compound 4th)

12th (compound 5th)

13th (compound 6th)

14th (compound 7th)

15th (compound 8ve or 2 8ves)

Each interval, both simple and compound, may be turned around. One may sing a perfect fifth (P5) up from C to G and a perfect fifth down from C to F. The latter is called singing the lower fifth.

Types of Intervals

Seconds, thirds, sixths, and sevenths may be major, minor, diminished, or augmented.*

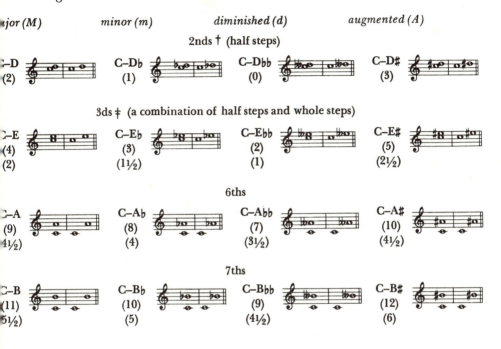

major (M)	minor (m)	diminished (d)	augmented (A)

2nds † (half steps)

| C–D (2) | C–Db (1) | C–Dbb (0) | C–D♯ (3) |

3ds ‡ (a combination of half steps and whole steps)

| C–E (4) (2) | C–Eb (3) (1½) | C–Ebb (2) (1) | C–E♯ (5) (2½) |

6ths

| C–A (9) (4½) | C–Ab (8) (4) | C–Abb (7) (3½) | C–A♯ (10) (4½) |

7ths

| C–B (11) (5½) | C–Bb (10) (5) | C–Bbb (9) (4½) | C–B♯ (12) (6) |

    * An oft-repeated, simple rule for remembering the classification of seconds, thirds, sixths, and sevenths goes something like this:

    major—if the upper note is in the major scale of the lower
    minor—if the upper note is in the minor scale of the lower
    augmented—if the upper note is larger than the major interval
    diminished—if the upper note is smaller than the minor interval.

This is a useful rule, but has its limitations, and as a matter of fact perpetuates a great fallacy since it allows for no such thing as a minor second. The note Db does not exist in either the major or the minor scale of C, yet C–Db is a minor second. Calling it a diminished second would actually be more logical. The German nomenclature of calling these four intervals either large (major) or small (minor) according to the number of half and whole steps the interval contains seems to be more accurate. This designation is quite important psychologically, for when one sings a major interval one should think in terms of "large," and conversely "small" when performing a minor interval. In this book, in order to conform with common practice, seconds, thirds, sixths, and sevenths will be labelled major (M), minor (m), diminished (d), or augmented (A), although the exercises are not necessarily based on the tonal system. Each interval must be studied and mastered by and for its own peculiar pitch characteristics.

    † Number of half steps in parentheses for each of the 2nds.

    ‡ For 3rds, 6ths, and 7ths, top numeral in parentheses gives the number of half steps, bottom numeral, the number of whole steps.

LEARNING ABOUT INTERVALS

Octaves, unisons, fourths, and fifths are called perfect (or pure), diminished, or augmented.

The octave or the unison (prime) cannot be altered at all, and these two intervals always have to be perfect, for as soon as one tampers with them they lose their unique characteristic. Theoretically or visually we will encounter such things as:

However, the instances are so rare and the alternate spellings used so frequently that not much time should be spent on these two intervals, except to say that the octave and the unison must almost always be perfect or pure, and if "imperfect" should be labelled (A) augmented or (d) diminished. The fourth and fifth are used a great deal in their enharmonic forms, so these must be easily and quickly identified.

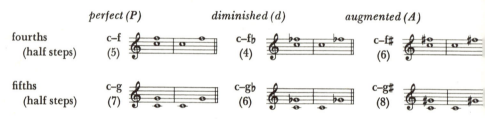

In this connection we must state that some intervals are merely "misspelled" for the sake of voice leading and other considerations. We call this an *enharmonic spelling*. Since C♯ and D♭ are the same note in our tempered scale, one has a different visual impression when seeing

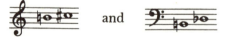

The first interval we would be correct to label M2, while the second should be designated as d3. Of course, the two intervals sound approximately the same.*

Enharmonic spellings, however, are important to many composers for harmonic considerations (such as the use of the augmented sixth

---

* The word "approximately" is used here to mollify any purists among us who may object to this statement. It is true that nontempered instruments such as strings and even the human voice may perform C♯ and D♭ with slight tonal variation, but for most ears and for our early attempts at sight singing, we must not concern ourselves too much with very small deviations.

and the diminished seventh), as well as for greater unity in voice leading, where the sharp is found in an ascending line and the flat for a descending one.

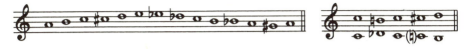

Exercises

1. Label each interval and include the number of half steps.

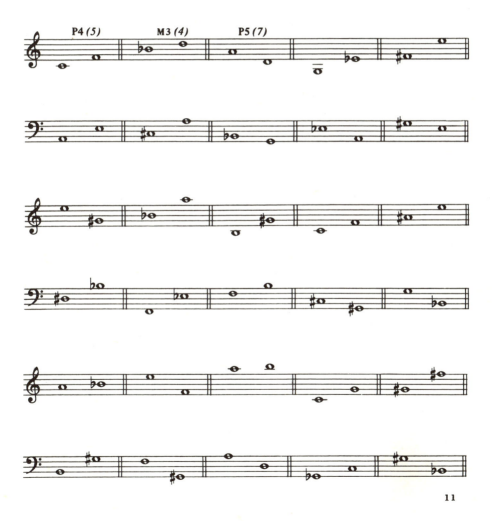

2. Fill in the missing pitch.

CHAPTER III

The Second

The object of both the melodic and rhythmic exercises in this book is to be able to read *all* music at sight. Even though it may seem rather tedious and even a bit unmusical at first, the task is worth pursuing, for the resulting facility is most desirable. When singing these non-rhythmic melodic examples you should strive to sing the intervals very slowly and perfectly in tune. Later on, when the intervallic relationships are firmly implanted in the ear, lines that make musical sense may be attempted at much faster and freer tempos. Therefore, the slurs, rests, and breathing signs are to be taken as suggestions and points of departure. New configurations may be built with these pitches to create many different melodies when new rhythms and other articulations are superimposed upon them. Such exercises will be found at the end of each of the chapters containing nonrhythmic exercises. You should then create your own "pieces" from the given notes contained in the nonrhythmic fragments. These may then be used as dictation exercises, dictated to you on your own instrument. This need not always be the piano, because, as has been suggested, you should be exposed to a variety of timbres, since this further sharpens aural perception.

Now each interval must be practiced separately so that a clear perception of its unique characteristics may be firmly established in the ear and so that it can be performed whenever it appears on a printed page. Each set of exercises is preceded by specific directions. Follow these very closely for best results. Do not skip around from a second to a fifth, for instance, but practice and master the intervals from small (seconds) to large (sevenths) in sequence, since some additive process takes place after the thirds are learned. In some of the later exercises for larger intervals (sixths and sevenths), some seconds and thirds are used. Therefore, these smaller intervals must be firmly implanted in the ear and the mind from the outset.

The Minor Second (m2)

The minor second is the smallest interval between two pitches. It is the "nearest" interval, only one half step in either direction.

Preparatory Exercises

Play the following minor seconds on the piano or any other "C" (nontransposing) instrument, then sing them. It is suggested that you sing each interval at least three times before going on to the next.

Nonrhythmic Exercises

Play the first note of each exercise on the piano, then try to sing through the entire exercise without accompaniment. Do it slowly at first, then increase speed with each successive repetition. A dash over a note means that it should be held a bit longer than the others.*

---

* If an exercise is out of your voice range, feel free to transpose it (as well as any passage or series of notes in this book) up or down an octave, but be sure that the intended intervals are maintained.

† Dot means a short note.

THE SECOND

Strike and Sing

Strike the notated pitch on the piano and then follow the instructions given. Do not play the pitch you are to sing on the piano until *after* you have sung it. The piano should be used only as a check of accuracy. Do these exercises very slowly and deliberately at first, then increase the speed gradually.

* Throughout this book, the accidental continues to apply if a pitch is repeated immediately and if there is no rest to separate the notes.

Strike, and sing a minor second above:

Strike, and sing a minor second below:

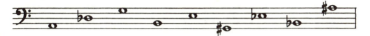

Strike, and sing the pitches indicated:

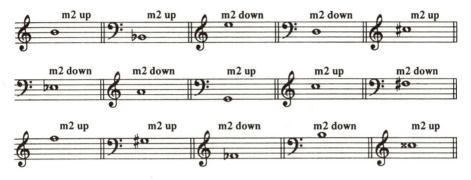

The Major Second (M2)

The major second is the distance of one whole step or two half steps between any two pitches.

Preparatory Exercises

As in the preparatory exercises for the minor second, play each of the following major seconds on the piano or any other "C" instrument, then sing. Repeat each example several times until the sound characteristic of this interval is well established in the ear.

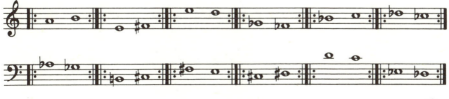

Nonrhythmic Exercises

Play the first note of each exercise on the piano, then sing the entire exercise without accompaniment. Slowly at first, then increase speed; remember, a dash over a note means that it should be held a bit longer than the others.

Combination of Major and Minor Seconds

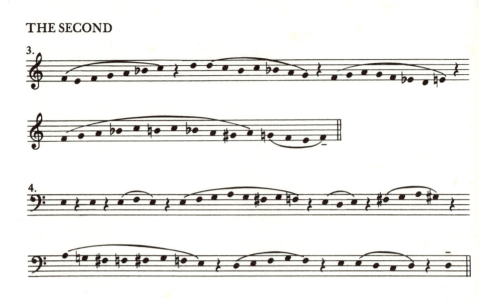

3.

4.

Strike and Sing

Strike the notated pitch on the piano and follow the instruction on each of the following exercises.

Strike, then sing a major second above:

Strike, then sing a major second below:

Strike, and sing the pitches indicated:

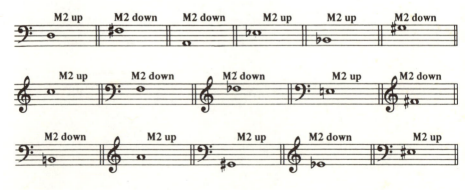

The Augmented Second (A2)

The augmented second is made up of three half steps or one whole plus one half step. Like other intervals discussed in later chapters, the augmented second is both an enharmonic and a psychological phenomenon. The fact that it is most often notated as a minor third lends it an enharmonic aspect, and we will practice it extensively in the next chapter where the minor third is dealt with. However, it is psychologically valid to include it here because many ethnic scales, especially Balkan, Near Eastern, and Jewish, feature an augmented second as an integral part of their melodic vocabulary.

"Hungarian major"

"Hungarian minor" (Ahavah Rabbah mode, Jewish)

Harmonically, this interval warrants our consideration. As we have seen, the harmonic minor scale contains an augmented second between the sixth and seventh scale degrees, since in common harmonic practice the leading tone must be present to form a major dominant seventh chord. So concerned were the original practitioners of our eighteenth–nineteenth-century harmonic system that they built strict admonitions into their voice-leading rules about avoiding the A2 by all means, since they felt that this interval, a bit like the tritone (A4, d5), was too difficult to perform. This may certainly be the case; however, today we can no longer avoid studying this interval as a separate entity, since we sing "world music," a great deal of which contains augmented seconds. Practice these few exercises as diligently as the others, for the interval appears here in ways that will be found in much of today's literature.

Preparatory Exercises

Play on the piano, then sing.

THE SECOND

Strike and Sing

Strike the notated pitch on the piano, then follow directions.

Strike and sing an augmented second below:

Strike and sing an augmented second above:

Nonrhythmic Exercises

Rhythmic Exercises

No dynamics will be indicated for these or subsequent rhythmic exercises in this book. Simply improvise your own after mastering each exercise.

THE SECOND

Simple Melodies Using Seconds

4.

5.

6.

7.

8.

CHAPTER IV

The Third

The Minor Third (m3)

The minor third is the interval of three half steps, or one whole step plus a half step. In the previous chapter, we were introduced to the augmented second, which also contains these two intervals; however, its usage was limited to scalewise progression, while the minor third "stands out by itself." It serves one of the most important and distinctive functions in all of Western music, since it distinguishes the major from the minor mode in tonal music of the past two to three hundred years.

Preparatory Exercises

Play on the piano, then sing. As in the previous chapter, it is suggested that each interval or group of intervals be sung several times after it is played.

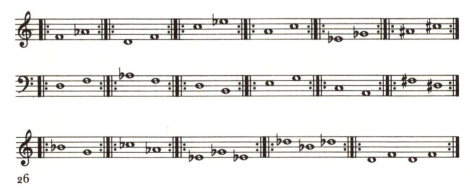

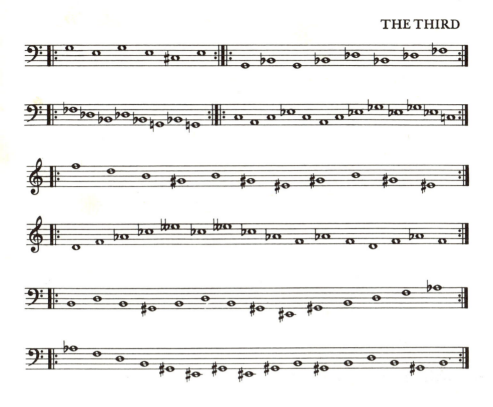

Strike and Sing

Strike the written note on the piano, and sing a minor third *above* it. When you finish the exercise, return to the beginning. Strike each note and sing a minor third *below* it.

THE THIRD

Strike the written note, then sing the pitch indicated.

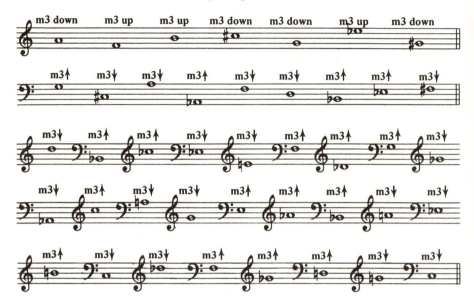

Nonrhythmic Exercises

Play first on an instrument, then try to sing the entire exercise without accompaniment, beginning slowly and gradually increasing the speed. Remember that the phrasing is only a suggestion, as are the dashes on pitches, which may be held a bit longer than the others.

The Major Third (M3)

The major third is the interval of four half steps, or two whole steps. Try to sing it "on the high side," for the major third is the "large" third and should be as high as one dares sing it. In this way, the pitch of an entire piece is helped. By "high," we do not mean sharp, but simply the psychological awareness of the difference between the minor third (small third) and the major third (large third).

THE THIRD

Preparatory Exercises

Play each group of pitches between repeat marks on the piano, then sing, repeating each formula at least three times.

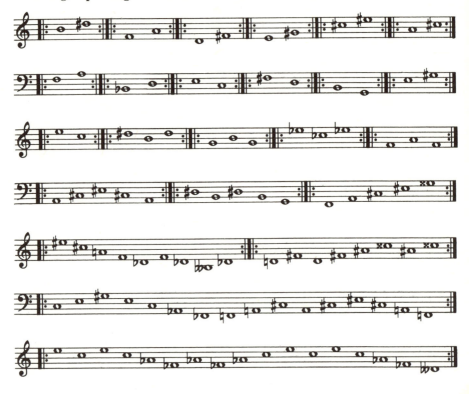

Strike and Sing

Strike the written note on the piano and sing a major third *above* each one. Then go back to the beginning, strike each note, and sing a major third *below* it.

Strike the written note and sing the pitch indicated.

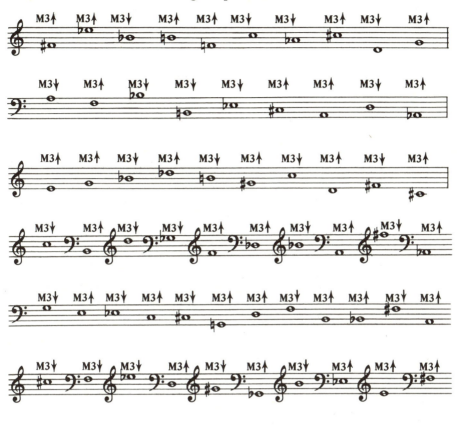

Nonrhythmic Exercises

Play the first note only, then try to sing without accompaniment. Check pitch after completing each exercise. (Be careful of enharmonic spellings!)

1.

THE THIRD

2.

3.

4.

5.

6.

Strike the written note and then sing the interval indicated. (Watch the mixed thirds carefully and tune the different thirds with precision.)

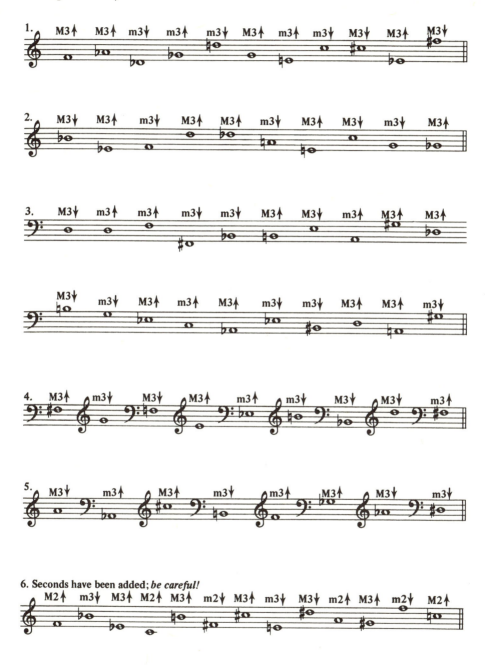

6. Seconds have been added; *be careful!*

Nonrhythmic Exercises

Mixed Major and Minor Thirds

Mixed Seconds and Thirds

2.

3.

4.

5.

6.

Rhythmic Exercises

1. Like a waltz

2. Quite fast

3. Stately

4. Smoothly flowing

5. **Moving quarters**

6.

7. **Dance like**

8. **Leisurely**

THE THIRD

9. Quite fast

10. Moderately fast

11. Happily

12. Quite slowly

The Diminished Fourth

Before we leave the study of thirds, we need to look at the "diminished fourth formula," which is an enharmonic spelling of the major third for the sake of good voice leading and the tonal implications in certain common practice harmonic progressions. Since you will encounter these quite frequently, practice this little exercise carefully, always remembering that the sound of the diminished fourth is, of course, the same as that of a major third.

Play on the piano, then sing, doing each formula three times:

For the harmonic execution of this melodic "d4 formula," sing as a class, or sing the soprano part and play the other three parts on the piano (altos watch the cross relations):

Sing as a class, or sing the bass part and play the other three:

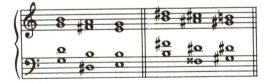

CHAPTER V

The Fourth and the Fifth

The Perfect Fourth (P4)

The perfect fourth is the interval of five half steps, or two whole and one half step. The word *perfect,* which is used to describe this interval and its inversion the perfect fifth (P5), stems from the fact that in tonal music these intervals remain constant even if the mode changes from major to minor or vice versa. In other languages they are sometimes referred to as "pure" fourths and fifths. Since they are inversions of one another, they are commonly grouped together. Moreover, the only independent altered fourth, the augmented fourth (A4), and the only independent altered fifth, the diminished fifth (D5), sound the same and are enharmonic spellings of the same-sounding interval called the *tritone* (three whole steps between any two intervals). They depend for their spelling on the resolution and proper voice leading of the two pitches.

Preparatory Exercises

Remember to play the interval or the group of intervals on the piano, and then sing without accompaniment.

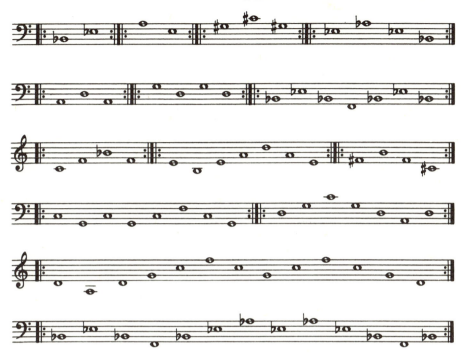

Strike and Sing

Strike the written note on the piano and sing a perfect fourth *below* it. Then go back to the beginning, strike each note, and sing a perfect fourth *above* it.

Strike the written note, then sing the pitch for which directions are given.

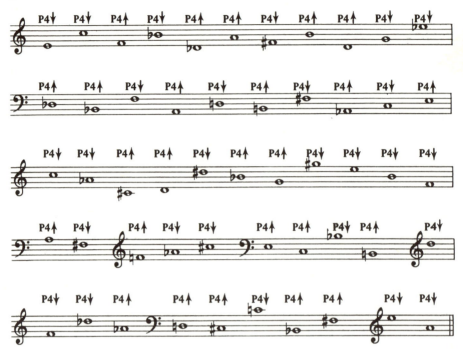

Nonrhythmic Exercises

Play on an instrument first, then sing entirely without accompaniment after the first note is sounded. (Check pitch at the end.)

While the nonrhythmic exercises in the previous chapters included only the interval being drilled, from here on, exercises of this type will make use of both smaller and larger intervals, in order to make them more singable. Now that you have completed Chapters III and IV, seconds and thirds of all types have been clearly established so that their use from now on aids further development in sight singing and ear training.

The Perfect Fifth (P5)

The perfect fifth is the interval of seven half steps, or three whole and one half step. It's importance stems from the fact that it is the first "new" note in the harmonic series after the unison and the octave; moreover, the first polyphonic system of Western music (organum) was based on this interval. "Tune" this interval well, for in our tempered scale system, the perfect fifth stabilizes the intonation of a piece of music to a great extent. We recognize that all strings tune to it or to the perfect fourth (double bass, etc.), and it becomes a most useful interval for tuning vocal music as well.

Preparatory Exercises

Remember to play the interval or the group of intervals on the piano, and then sing without accompaniment.

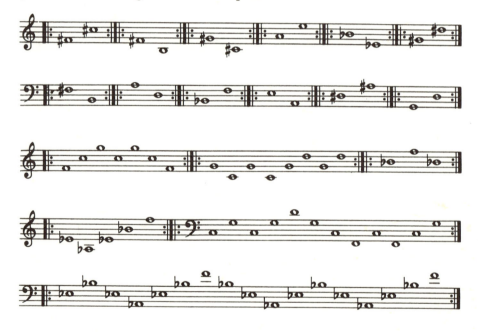

Strike and Sing

Strike the written note on the piano and sing a perfect fifth *above* each one. Then go back to the beginning, strike each note, and sing a perfect fifth *below* it.

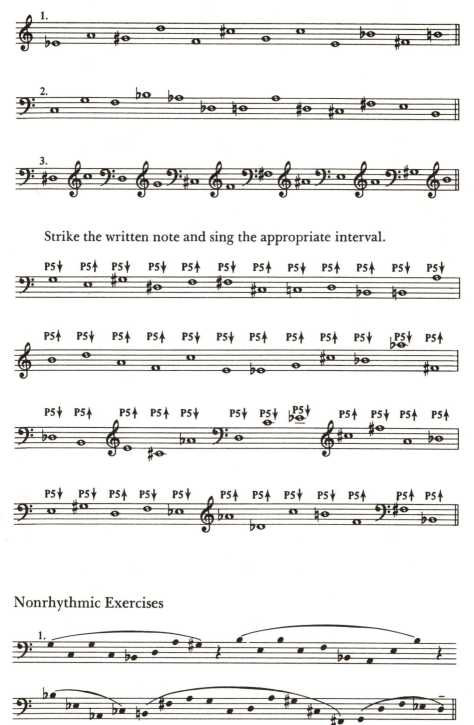

Strike the written note and sing the appropriate interval.

Nonrhythmic Exercises

THE FOURTH AND THE FIFTH

Special Exercise for Mixed P4 and P5

Sing each group at least three times, giving the starting pitch on the piano.

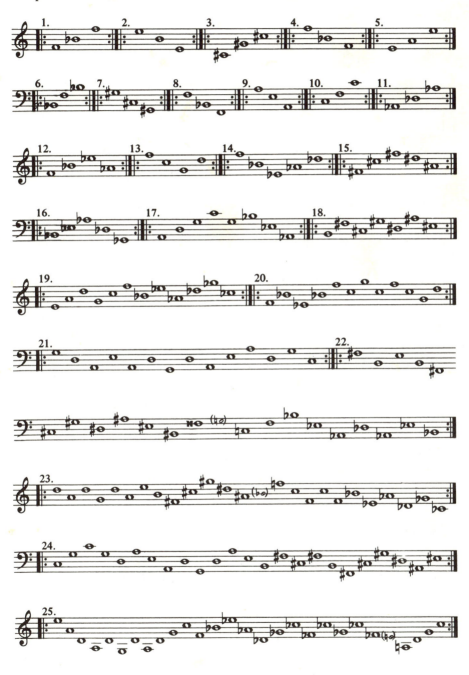

The Tritone (A4 or d5)

The augmented fourth or the diminished fifth, called the *tritone,* is six half steps or three whole steps between any two pitches. It is not invertible. Because it sounded awkward and was certainly hard to sing, it was banned in plainsong and in early polyphonic music, and was called *diabolus in musica,* the devil in music. Even in the common practice period on which much of our harmony and counterpoint exercises are based, we find rules and prohibitions concerning this interval. Within the diatonic style, it is a restless interval always needing resolution. The spellings making a tritone, either A4 or d5, stem from this "restless" quality and depend on the resolution of the tritone in this manner:

Preparatory Exercises

Remember to play the interval or group of intervals on the piano, and then sing without accompaniment.

Strike and Sing

Strike the written note on the piano and sing a tritone *above* each one. Then go back to the beginning, strike each note, and sing a tritone *below* it.

Strike the written note and sing the interval indicated in the directions.

THE FOURTH AND THE FIFTH

Nonrhythmic Exercises

Predominantly Tritones

Predominantly Mixed Fourths, Fifths, and Tritones

Rhythmic Exercises

1. Moderately fast

2. As fast as possible

3. Rather slowly

4. **Quite fast** *(all separate notes staccato)*

5. Very slowly

6. Lightly moving (in 1)

7. Deliberately

THE FOURTH AND THE FIFTH

8. Fast

9. Moving sprightly along

p (echo-like)

10. Slowly

Canons

JOHANNES BRAHMS

Allegretto *(4 parts)*

Repeat three times

* 4, 3, 2, 1 stop at these fermatas at the third repeat.

LUIGI CHERUBINI

Happily *(3 parts)*

Repeat three times

55

THE FOURTH AND THE FIFTH

JOHANNES BRAHMS

Andante espressivo *(4 parts)*

Repeat three times

PAUL HINDEMITH

Smoothly moving *(3 parts)*

Repeat three times

JOHANNES BRAHMS

Andante con moto *(4 parts)*

Repeat three times

* 4, 3, 2, 1, stop at fermatas at the third repeat.

56

* 4, 3, 2, 1 stop at these fermatas at the third repeat.

57

THE FOURTH AND THE FIFTH

EUSEBIUS MANDYCZEWSKI

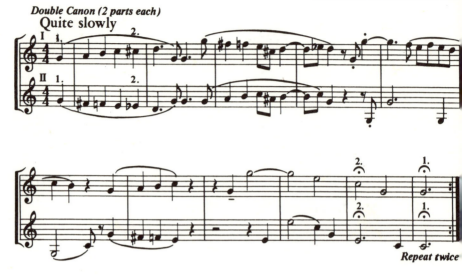

The fermatas are the stopping places for the respective voices the second time through.

CHAPTER VI

The Sixth

The Minor Sixth (m6)

The minor sixth is the interval of eight half steps, or four whole steps. Here we enter the major-minor tonal system again, if only by the designation of the intervals themselves. It has often been suggested that intervals larger than the fifth ought to be heard as "compound" intervals. This would mean that the best way to remember the minor sixth would be to sing a perfect fourth followed by a minor third:

However, this method eclipses the basic independence of each interval. It is therefore suggested that you carefully, diligently, and slowly practice the sixths in this chapter and the sevenths in the next chapter as independent intervals, being attentive at all times to their tonal individualities and characteristics, and integrating each interval as a separate entity into your auditory vocabulary.

THE SIXTH

Preparatory Exercises

As before, play each fragment on the piano and sing it repeatedly.

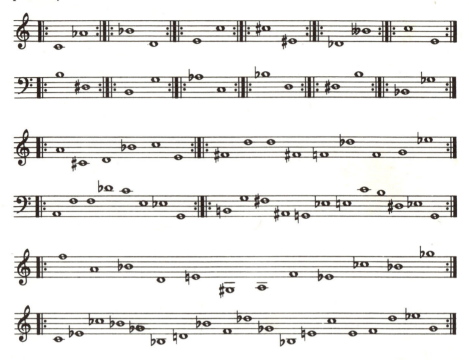

Strike and Sing

Strike the written note on the piano and sing a m6 below each one.

Strike the written note on the piano and sing a m6 above each one.

Strike the written note, then sing the interval indicated by the direction above each note.

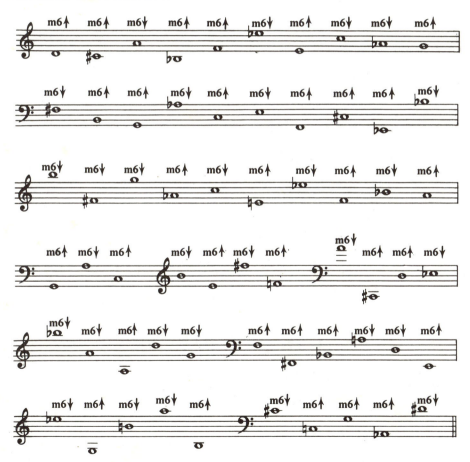

THE SIXTH

Nonrhythmic Exercises

The Major Sixth (M6)

The major sixth is the interval of nine half steps, or four whole steps plus a half step. As in the case of the major third and the major seventh, the major sixth is the "large sixth," and great care must therefore be taken to sing it as high as one dares in order to ensure the difference between the minor and major sixth.

Preparatory Exercises

Do not forget to repeat each fragment several times, until the sound is well implanted in the ear.

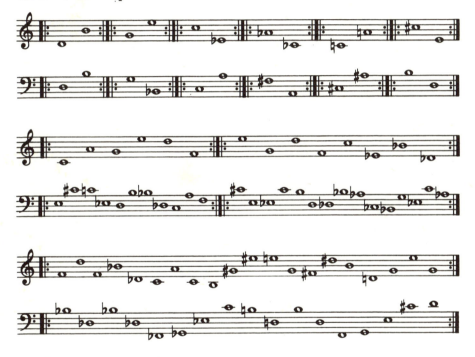

Strike and Sing

Strike the written note on the piano, then sing a M6 above each one.

THE SIXTH

Strike the written note on the piano, then sing a M6 below each one.

Strike the written note, then sing the interval indicated in the directions above each note.

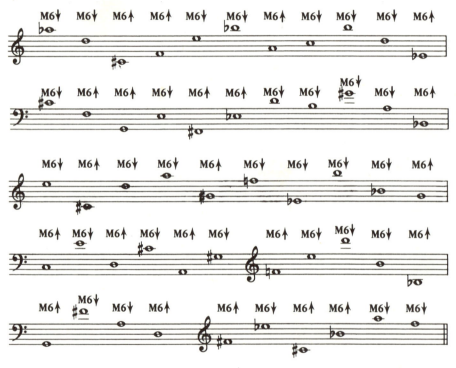

Nonrhythmic Exercises

Mixed Sixths

Again a warning is in order: the student should be very careful to distinguish between the two sixths by feeling the unique qualities of the small (m6) and the large (M6) one. Although this sense of difference may be purely psychological, it will insure good intonation.

Preparatory Exercises

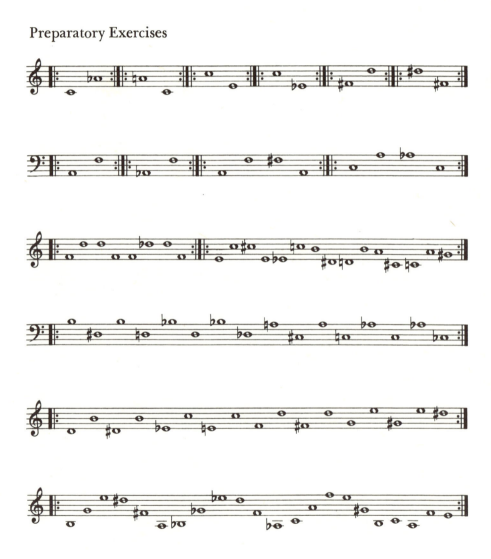

Strike and Sing

Strike the written note, then sing the interval indicated above each one.

Nonrhythmic Exercises

Rhythmic Exercises

1. **Fast**

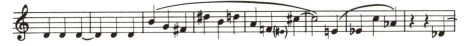

2. **Gently rocking**

3. **Stately**

THE SIXTH

4. Quite fast

5. Happily

6. Slowly

7. As fast as it can be done comfortably

8. Slowly and relaxed

9. Fast

10. Very slowly

The Augmented Sixth

This chapter would not be complete without a brief discussion of the augmented sixth. Although it is an enharmonic spelling of the minor seventh, its use in the augmented sixth chords which occur so frequently in common practice harmony makes it necessary to look at this phenomenon before you practice the seventh intervals. You will actually practice the interval in the next chapter, but play the following exercises on the piano to see how it functions.

Most commonly used A6 chords

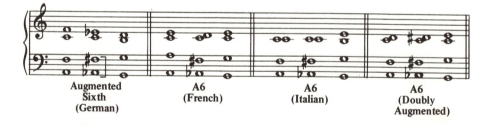

Conversely, the interval called a diminished seventh is actually an enharmonically spelled major sixth. This respelling is necessitated by its resolution in the tonal idiom, since a sharped note rises and a flatted note moves downward.

In both cases, the augmented sixth as well as the diminished seventh are most important visually and psychologically, for they determine upward or downward movement in tonal music.

Harmonic and melodic use of the d7

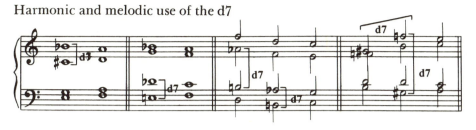

Canons

Most of the canons presented in this and other chapters were written on non-English texts. Rather than risk inadequate or unmusical translation, we have often chosen to omit the text altogether so that you may concentrate on the interval content and perform the music accurately. Even those canons that have been translated would benefit from performance with neutral syllables. Each canon should be studied in unison and then divided up into parts once the lines can be performed with ease.

LUDWIG VAN BEETHOVEN, *It Must Be*

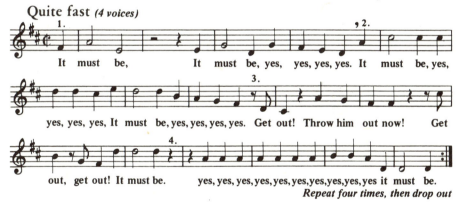

Repeat four times, then drop out

LUDWIG VAN BEETHOVEN, *Cool, Not Lukewarm* *

Repeat three times, then drop out

* A canon whose text is a pun on the name of the composer Friedrich Kuhlau: *kühl* (cool), *nicht* (not), *lau* (lukewarm).

† In German, *B* signifies B♭; *H,* B♮. We do not know if the use of the notes B♭–A–C–B♮ (or, in German, B–A–C–H) was an intentional allusion to the composer's name.

73

THE SIXTH

FRIEDRICH KUHLAU, *Anti-Cherubini* ‡

‡ A canon intending to extoll the virtues of lesser composers, who used clear and singable material, as opposed to Luigi Cherubini's chromaticism.

FRANZ SCHUBERT, *Welcome to the Month of May*

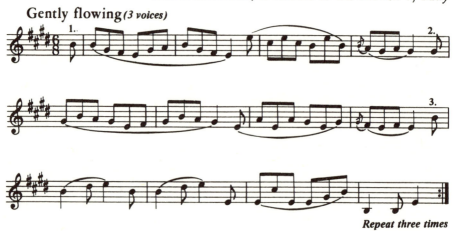

GEORG TELEMANN, *O Lord, How Long (Psalm 13)*

WOLFGANG AMADEUS MOZART, *Ave Maria*

DONA NOBIS PACEM *(Attributed to Mozart)*

Repeat three times

ROBERT SCHUMANN, *A Drinking Song*

Repeat three times

JOSQUIN DES PREZ, *Pleni sunt coeli*

(2 voices)

Ple - ni sunt coe - - - - li, ple - ni sunt coe - - li et ter - ra, et ter - ra glo - ri - a, glo - ri - a_____ tu - a,_____ glo - ri - a_____ tu - a, glo - ri - a_____ tu - a_____

rit.

(No repeat)

ANON. *(sixteenth century), Confide filia*

(4 voices)

Con-fi-de fi - li - a, fi-des tu - a te_ sal - - vam fe - cit, te sal-vam fe - cit. Con-fi-de fi - li - a, con-fide fi-li - a fi - li - a.

1., 2., 3. **last ending**

Repeat four times

CHAPTER VII

The Seventh

The Minor Seventh (m7)

The minor seventh is the interval of ten half steps, or five whole steps. Like many of the intervals discussed earlier, the minor seventh is of great importance to the entire tonal system because it is a member of the dominant seventh chord, which consists of one major third and

two minor thirds: m7 . This chord, and therefore the interval

itself, demands resolution in this tonal context. However, we shall study and practice the minor seventh for its own particular qualities, so that if we meet it in nontonal surroundings (i.e., much of the music of the twentieth century), it will present no difficulty regardless of whether it is resolved or not, whether it is preceded or followed by another minor seventh or by an even more tense (dissonant) interval. In the course of these exercises, we shall be made aware of the many different combinations of intervals which may be contained within the minor seventh, such as two perfect fourths, a perfect fifth and a minor third, etc. These combinations should be practiced with great care so that they may serve as guiding outlines, where needed, to "tune" the minor seventh well.

Preparatory Exercises

Play fragments several times, then sing them repeatedly until each is mastered.

THE SEVENTH

Strike and Sing

Strike the written note on the piano, then sing a minor seventh above each one.

Strike the written note on the piano, then sing a minor seventh below each one.

Strike the written note, then sing the interval indicated in the directions above each note.

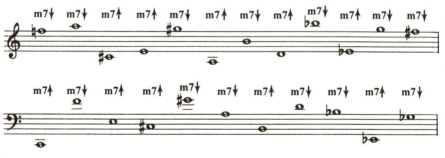

Nonrhythmic Exercises

The Major Seventh (M7)

The major seventh is the interval of eleven half steps, or five and one half whole steps. This interval has been called "the contemporary composer's disease," because it has become one of the most frequently used intervals in the music of the twentieth century. Its use as a melodic interval before the twentieth century was rare and always created a situation that needed resolution. Today, consecutive sevenths, both melodic and harmonic, are most commonplace and create the kind of tension in which contemporary composers are often interested. The major seventh is the interval of greatest tension within an octave; practice it carefully, but do *not* use "the octave down a half step" as a crutch.

Preparatory Exercises

Play, then sing repeatedly.

THE SEVENTH

Strike and Sing

Strike the written note on the piano, then sing a major seventh above each one.

Strike the written note on the piano, then sing a major seventh below each one.

Strike the written note, then sing the interval indicated in the directions above each note.

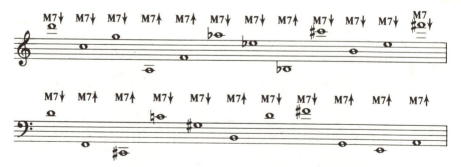

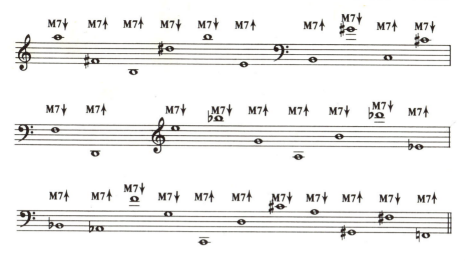

Nonrhythmic Exercises

Mixed Sevenths

It is important to remember that there is a large (major) and a small (minor) seventh and to differentiate between them carefully, since pitch suffers greatly from the mistuning of any intervals, especially the large ones.

Preparatory Exercises

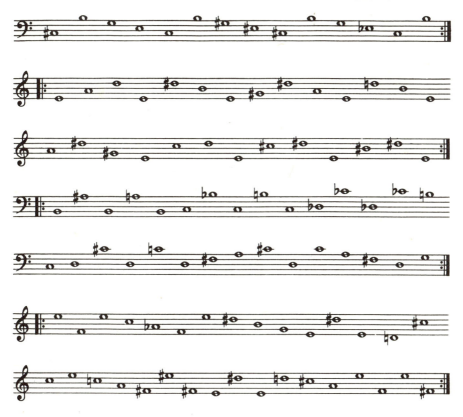

Strike and Sing

Strike the written note, then sing the interval indicated, following the directions above each note.

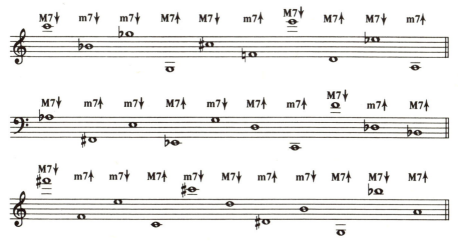

THE SEVENTH

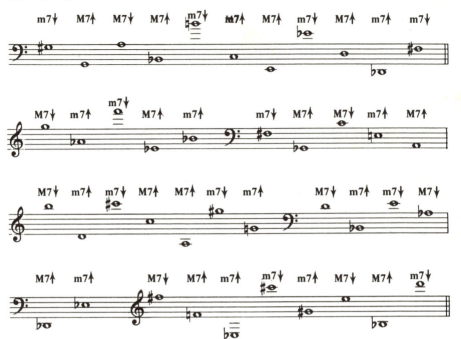

Nonrhythmic Exercises

7.

8.

Rhythmic Exercises

1. **Happily**

THE SEVENTH

5. Stately

6. Quite fast

7. Quite slowly

8. Moderately moving (in slow 2)

9. Like a waltz

10. Rather slowly and leisurely

Canons

MICHAEL PRAETORIUS, *Viva la musica*

Vi - va, vi - va la mu-si - ca. Vi - va, vi - va la mu-si - ca. Vi - va la mu-si - ca.

Repeat three times

JOHANN STADEN, *All Who Hate Music Are Not Worthy of Hearing It*

Repeat seven times

PAUL SARTORIUS, *Music, The Dispeller of Sorrows*

Repeat four times

LUDWIG GEBHARDI, *Glory to God*

Glo - ry to God in the high - est. Peace___ on earth___ and good

will, and good will to - ward all men. A - - men.___

Repeat four times

* The fermatas in these canons signify the stopping places when the first voice has sung the entire canon the final time.

94

GIAMBATTISTA MARTINI, *A New Hymn*

FRANZ JOSEPH HAYDN, *Solid Truth*

WOLFGANG AMADEUS MOZART, *Lacrimoso*

95

THE SEVENTH

JOHANNES BRAHMS, *Lullaby*

Repeat three times

JOHANNES BRAHMS, *A Pretty Bird Sits in a Tree*

CHARLES GOUNOD, *Parting*

Repeat four times

FRANZ LACHNER, *When I Know What You Know*

Repeat three times

ANON., *As the Dew Awakens a Wilting Flower*

Repeat four times

ANON., *Hallelujah*

Repeat three times

ANON., *Two All-Interval Canons*

I

Repeat three times

II

Repeat three times

97

THE SEVENTH

Three Original Canons

CHAPTER VIII

Scales and Chords

In this chapter, we shall discuss scales and other passages less frequently utilized than the major/minor configurations which have dominated our music for over three hundred years. Some of these patterns are becoming more and more commonplace today, and many were very popular during the Middle Ages and the Renaissance. As far as the chords are concerned, we shall practice patterns that are rather unusual when compared to the traditional chord vocabulary. However, many composers today build chords on intervals vastly different from the stacked thirds with which we have dealt for so long.

Modal Scales and Passages

Play the first note of each scale or exercise on an instrument, then sing. Check the notes after the exercise has been repeated at least three times.

SCALES AND CHORDS

Dorian

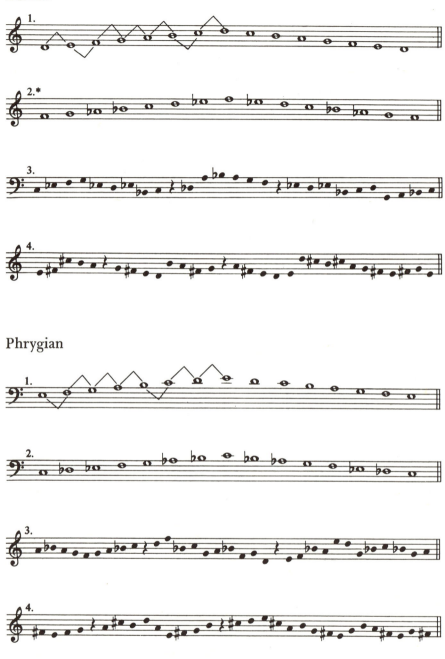

Phrygian

* You may begin a modal scale or a synthetic scale on any scale step, but you must, of course, be careful to use the prescribed pattern of half and whole steps of the particular scale.

Lydian

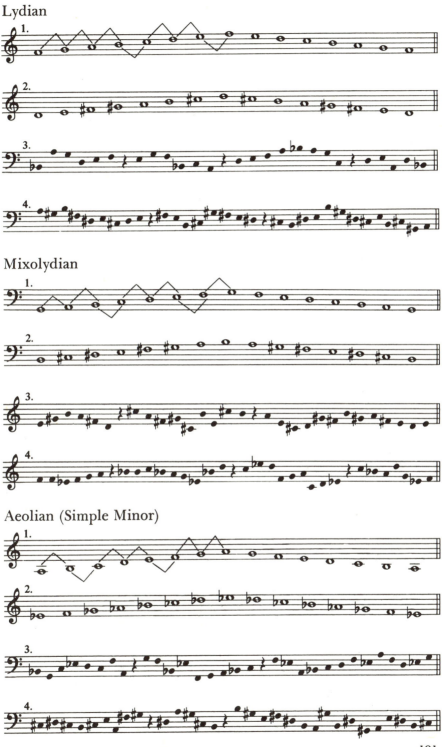

Mixolydian

Aeolian (Simple Minor)

Locrian

Other Scales

Repeat each of the following scales at least three times—slowly at first, then increase speed.

The Chromatic Scale

The Whole-Tone Scale

Synthetic or "Hybrid" Scales

   Caution: Sing these patterns purely by interval. Do *not* rely on second guessing!

SCALES AND CHORDS

Alter or rearrange the circled pitches at least six different ways, then sing them. The "new" scales may also be used for dictation exercises.

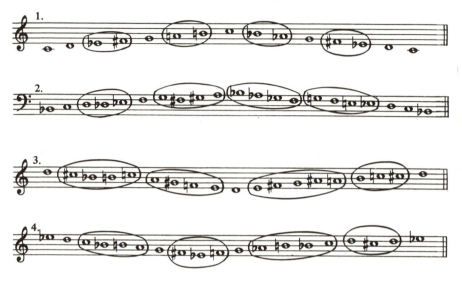

Like-Interval Chords

Sing each chord series at the pitch given, then select three additional starting pitches and sing the transposed series.

Major Thirds

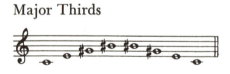

Class sings: First the women, then the men; then together. Finally, mix up the parts.

Minor Thirds

Class sings:

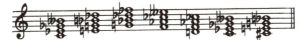

Perfect Fourths

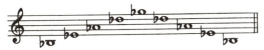

Class sings:

Perfect Fifths

Class sings:

Tritones (A4, d5)

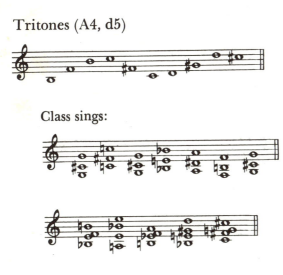

Class sings:

SCALES AND CHORDS

Minor Sixths

Class sings:

Major Sixths

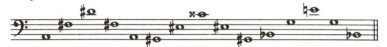

Class sings:

Minor Seventh

Class sings:

Major Seventh

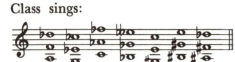

Class sings:

Diverse-Interval Chords

In the following paired exercises, first sing the top line—broken chords—three times. Then sing the chords in the next line as broken chords (arpeggios), both up and down. Finally, if a class is present, sing these same chords as unbroken chords, progressing directly from one to another.

Sing these chords very slowly:

Planing (or Paralleling) Exercises

These are to be executed in two ways at least, choosing any of the chords above: 1a, 2a, or 3a.

Example

etc.

You should also try to sequence chromatically or in thirds, etc.

etc.

Try these "paralleling" exercises as a class:

etc.

or

etc.

Other Clefs

Throughout our studies in intervallic reading thus far, we have limited ourselves to music in the bass or treble clef. Historically, many clefs have been employed in each period to serve the needs of the instruments and the music then current. In our time, there are at least two additional clefs which are frequently used: the *alto clef,* in which middle C is notated on the third line:

and the *tenor clef,* in which middle C is notated on the fourth line:

Why should we study these clefs? Because they do occur with fair frequency in music being written and performed today. The alto clef is used to notate most music for the viola and may also be found in eighteenth- and nineteenth-century scores that include the alto trombone. The tenor clef is often used to notate the higher register of the cello, the double bass, the bassoon, and the tenor trombone.

Exercises

Write the equivalent note in either treble or bass clef on the lower line:

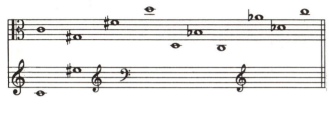

Write out these lines in the bass and treble clefs:

SCALES AND CHORDS

Sing the following lines:

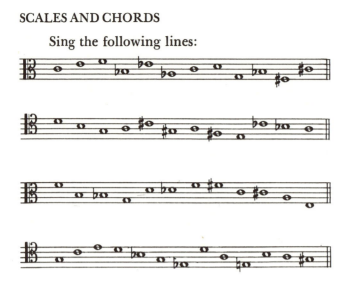

Strike and Sing

Quite often, it is difficult to assimilate a pitch that is displaced radically from one's own singing range. Therefore, study these exercises most slowly and carefully. Transpose the "out-of-range" pitches into your own vocal range, of course:

Strike each of the following notes on the piano and sing in the directions indicated:

1. a major second up:

2. a minor second down:

3. a perfect fifth up:

4. a perfect fourth down:

5. a major second down:

6. a minor second up:

7. a major third up:

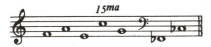

8. a minor third down:

9. a perfect fourth up:

10. a minor third up:

11. a perfect fifth up:

12. a major sixth up:

13. a tritone (augmented fourth or diminished fifth) down:

14. a major seventh up:

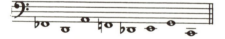

15. a minor seventh down:

16. a minor sixth up:

17. a major seventh down:

18. a major sixth down:

19. a minor seventh up:

20. a minor sixth down:

21. a major third down:

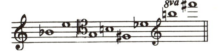

22. Strike C and sing this row of random intervals:

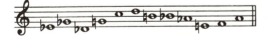

23. Take this one from dictation (strike C before beginning):

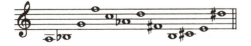

24. another row of random intervals to sing (strike C again):

25. a final row to sing (strike C):

CHAPTER IX

Melodies for Practice and Review

Preparatory Exercises

In order to review all the intervals in their different relationships to one another, work on these fifteen preliminary exercises very slowly and carefully. Sound the first pitch of each exercise on an instrument, then sing the example without accompaniment several times, always checking the final pitch to see that it is correct.

MELODIES FOR PRACTICE AND REVIEW

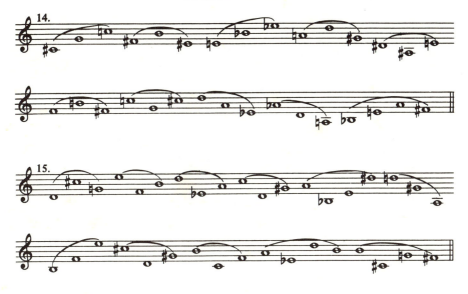

Forty-Two Twentieth-Century Melodies

Each melody should be worked out in the following manner:

1. nonrhythmically;
2. very slowly, but rhythmically;
3. rhythmically and up to tempo.

Nonrhythmic version of the first melody:

SAMUEL BARBER, Overture to *The School for Scandal*

1. **Quietly moving**

MELODIES FOR PRACTICE AND REVIEW

ROY HARRIS, *Third Symphony*

2. **Slowly**

BÉLA BARTÓK, *Concerto for Orchestra, IV*

3. **Calmo** ♩ = 108

PAUL HINDEMITH, *Mathis der Maler, I*

4. **Quite fast**

BENJAMIN BRITTEN, *Serenade*

5. **Alla marcia**

IGOR STRAVINSKY, *Petrushka, Fourth Tableau,*
Dance of the Nursemaids

6. **Lively**

ARNOLD SCHOENBERG, *String Quartet No. 4, I*

7. **Fast**

MELODIES FOR PRACTICE AND REVIEW

ARNOLD SCHOENBERG, *Wind Quintet, III*

8. Slowly

ALBAN BERG, Excerpts from *Lulu*

9.

10.

11.

12.

13.

14.

15.

16.

17.

18.

19.

20.

21.

22.

23.

24.

25.

26. Fast

27. Slowly

28.

29.

30.

BENJAMIN BRITTEN, *Elegy from Serenade*

31. Slowly

SAMUEL BARBER, *The Queen's Face on the Summery Coin*

32. Moderato

SAMUEL BARBER, *I Hear an Army*

33. Allegro

PAUL HINDEMITH, *Over the Breast of Spring*

34. Slow

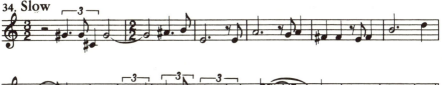

PAUL HINDEMITH, *Vor der Passion* from *Das Marienleben*

35. Very slowly

CHARLES IVES, *A Sea Dirge*

36. In a slow swaying way

AARON COPLAND, *In the Beginning*

37. Slowly

DAVID DI CHIERA, *Black Bead*

38.

MELODIES FOR PRACTICE AND REVIEW

IRVING FINE, *Polavoli*

BÉLA BARTÓK, *Lost Content*

ANTON WEBERN, *Cantata No. 1, I*

MELODIES FOR PRACTICE AND REVIEW

ANTON WEBERN, *Cantata No. 2, I*

42.

PART TWO

Rhythmic Studies

CHAPTER X

Definition of Rhythmic Terms

Music, like dance, is basically a temporal art. That means it is dependent to a great extent on the dimension of time, through which it passes. The way we organize music within a temporal, rather than spatial, framework is called *rhythm*. The word comes from the Greek *rhythmos*, meaning flow or continuity. Plato said, "Rhythm is ordered movement." Some other standard dictionary definitions may help us further to understand this important concept:

Rhythm is the organization of pitches in recognizable patterns.
Rhythm is a "periodic quality"—the regular and irregular of all musical movement.
Rhythm in the broadest sense is the organization of duration.

One isolated, nonrepeated sound cannot constitute a rhythm; however, it can become a unit of a rhythmic phrase. This single unit of duration is called a *pulse* or a *beat*.

The organization of pulses into groups of twos, threes, fours, etc., is called *meter*. Meter is achieved by placing a *stress* or an *accent* on the first pulse of each pattern. By accents, we do not always mean a beat that is louder or stronger than the others or one that always constitutes the first beat of a pattern. Yet without some kind of accents, whether regular or irregular, notes become simply a "monotonous series of pulse-groups," as Paul Creston puts it. What we mean by a musical accent is any kind of emphasis on a beat or pitch that makes it stressed or more pronounced than the rest of the pattern.

There are three basic ways of achieving the feeling of accent in a pulse grouping, notwithstanding the natural tendency to group irregular as well as regular sounds into patterns of twos and threes (for example, the ticking of a clock or a hammering outside our door). They are:

    1. *Dynamic accent*—performing a note louder than the others:

WOLFGANG AMADEUS MOZART, Overture to *The Magic Flute*

    2. *Agogic accent*—making a note longer than the others:

LUDWIG VAN BEETHOVEN, *Ninth Symphony, IV*

    3. *Tonic* or *pitch accent*—having one note higher than the others:

FELIX MENDELSSOHN, *Fourth Symphony, I*

    There are other ways of achieving accentuation, for instance by harmonic or textural weight—i.e., harmonizing one note with a greater dissonance or with greater density of texture than the others. This is called either *harmonic accent* or *weight accent*. Another accent is called the *embellishment accent* because it is the embellishment or the ornamentation that calls attention to the particular note.

FRANZ JOSEPH HAYDN, *Symphony No. 103, III*

The metric groups of beats, with the first beat usually accented either strongly or sometimes almost imperceptibly by any of the above means, are called *measures*. These are separated from each other by *barlines*. A *measure* or a *bar* may be called the distance between two barlines.

The speed with which the beats occur or are performed in music is called *tempo*. At the beginning of a piece of music, we may find a verbal description of the speed or tempo at which it is to be performed, or a precise metronome marking. The metronome marking indicates how many pulses or beats are to occur within every minute of a particular movement or passage. For example, the indication ♩ = 48 means that the piece is to be played slowly, for only 48 beats (in this case 48 quarter notes) should occur in the course of a minute. On the other hand, a passage marked ♩ = 138 will be played fast, since 138 quarter notes must be fitted into 60 seconds. The marking ♩ = 60 can be tested without a metronome, for the unit specified (here a quarter note) will have a duration of one second and may be regulated by a watch.

In older music, the character of the music and its notation determine the tempo, but this is a matter with which we will not concern ourselves at this moment. As for tempo indication by verbal description, we must rely on our own perception of the music and how to achieve greatest clarity of performance. It is suggested that if there is no metronome marking, the performer gauge his consideration of speed on the smallest units of notation and calculate at what speed these fast notes would be most clearly defined. Similarly, in a slow piece, the small units must not sound rushed, yet must convey the feeling of movement and "inner beat" which is so necessary in giving a slow work clarity, intensity, and vitality.

FRANZ JOSEPH HAYDN, *Symphony No. 99, I*

In the example above, tempo must be determined by the speed with which the sixteenth notes can be performed with clarity. Otherwise, the work takes on a frantic quality.

J. S. BACH, *Cantata No. 140*

In this Bach excerpt, the thirty-second notes must be the measuring rod. Although the piece bears a slow marking, Adagio, the eighth notes must be steady yet must not drag. Therefore, the thirty-second notes must not be played so fast that they give any kind of frantic feeling to this noble and rather pastoral piece.

Table of Rhythmic Values

The student should get this table of rhythmic values firmly implanted in his mind so that reading rhythmic notation will become second nature during the course of this study.

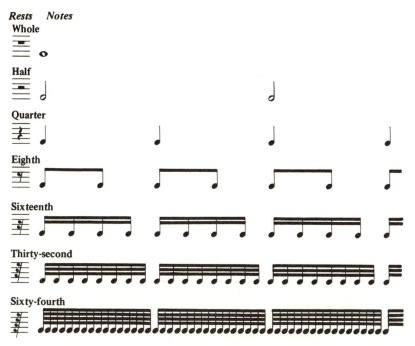

Whole = 2 half = 4 quarter = 8 eighth = 16 sixteenth = 32 thirty-second = 64 sixty-fourth notes

A dot following any note elongates it by *one half* of its own value.

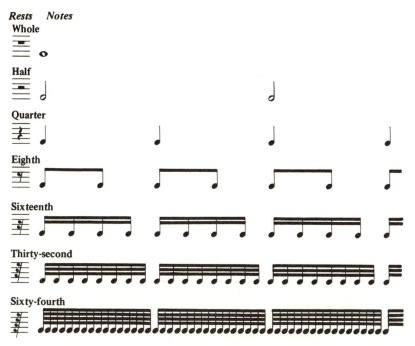

Less frequently, we encounter a note followed by two dots. This elongates the note by half the value of the note plus half the value of the first dot. These are the most frequently encountered double-dotted note values:

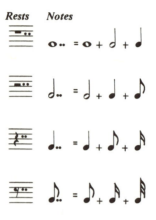

Nonmeasured Rhythmic Exercises

The rhythmic or time signature is usually constructed of two numbers. The upper number signifies the number of beats in a single measure; the lower number tells the unit of measurement. The signature $\frac{3}{4}$ indicates that there are three quarter notes in a measure, while $\frac{7}{8}$ signifies that seven eighth notes make up the measure. For our first exercises, only the unit measurement (lower number) is considered, so that $\frac{x}{4}$ will mean a quarter note gets a beat, or $\frac{x}{8}$ an eighth note, etc.

In the following exercises:

a. Set a metronome on 60 and let each basic unit equal one "click" of the metronome; then perform the exercises. (If no metronome is available, use a watch or clap a steady pulse equal to a unit note per second.)

b. In the classroom, one half of the class may clap a steady beat, while the other half performs the exercises.

c. If a metronome setting of 60 (or one unit per second) is too fast, begin by selecting a slower tempo and gradually work up to 60 and, eventually faster.

d. Repeat each exercise at least three times.

e. Use the syllable *ta* or *doo,* so that the articulation of each note is very clear.

♩ = 60

1.

2.

3.

4.

5.

6.

With rests (clap hands for the rests):

7.

8.

9.

10.

RHYTHMIC TERMS

Simple (Common) Meter

Simple Duple Meter, the "Two-Beat"

Measures in duple meter contain two beats: $\frac{2}{4}$, $\frac{2}{2}$, $\frac{2}{8}$. These are the most commonly used two-beat meters, and of these, we will probably encounter $\frac{2}{4}$ more frequently than the others. Practice all three in order to familiarize yourself with problems of smaller and larger rhythmic values.

Preparatory Exercises

Repeat each fragment several times, always conducting the "two" pattern until it feels natural. Then proceed to the regular duple meter exercises. For both preliminary and regular exercises, begin rather slowly, approximately ♩ = 60, 𝅗𝅥 = 60, or ♪ = 60 (the basic unit = 60) increasing the speed each time you complete an exercise until you reach an eventual speed of ♩ = 120, 𝅗𝅥 = 120, ♪ = 120 (the basic unit = 120).

SIMPLE (COMMON) METER

1. 

2. 

3. 

4. 

5. 

6. 

7. 

8. 

9. 

10. 

11. 

12. 

Regular Exercises

All exercises should be conducted while they are performed.

1. 

2. 

3. 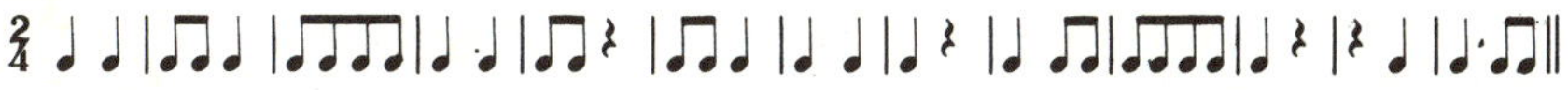

4. 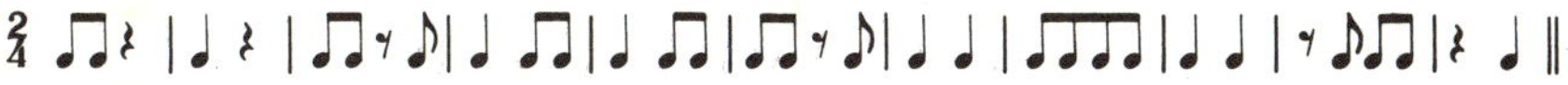

5. 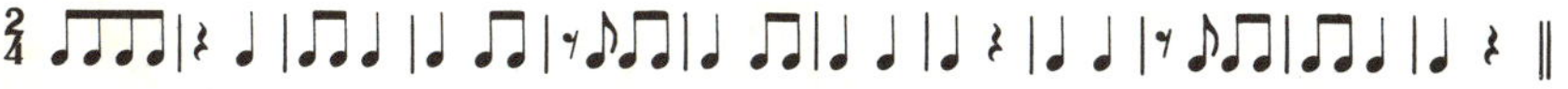

6. 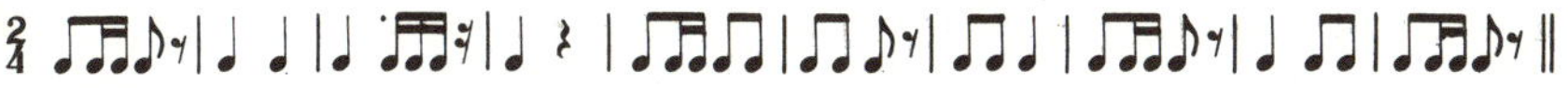

7. 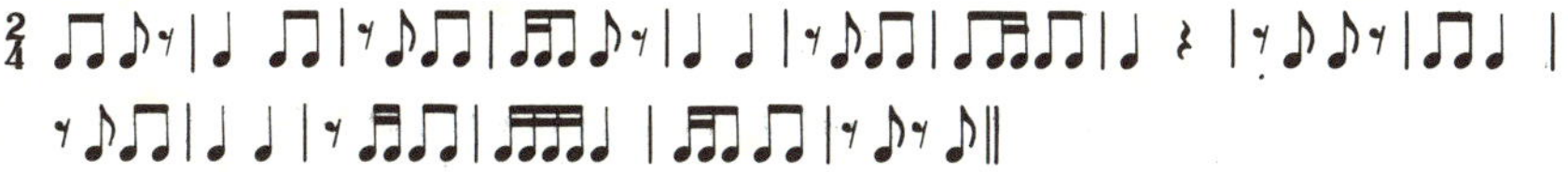

8. 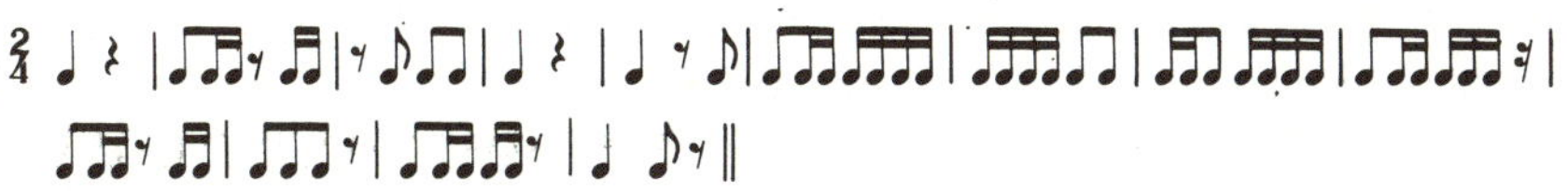

9. 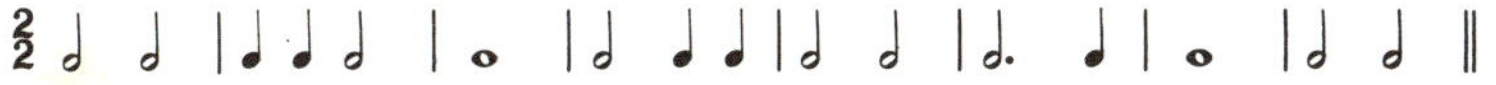

10. 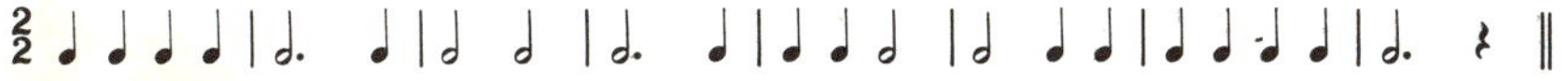

11. 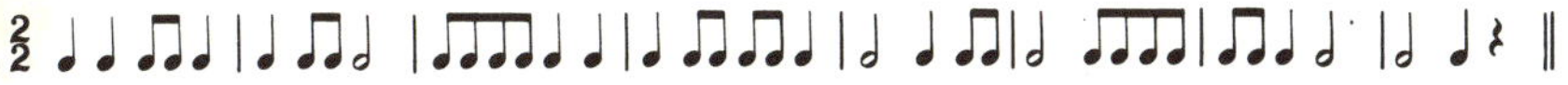

12. 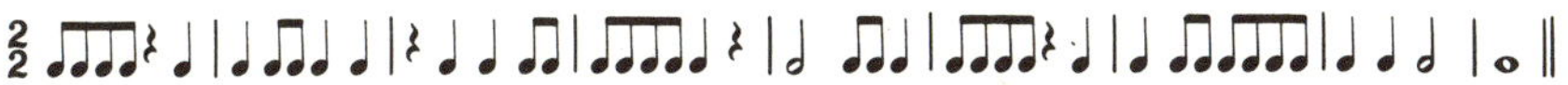

13. 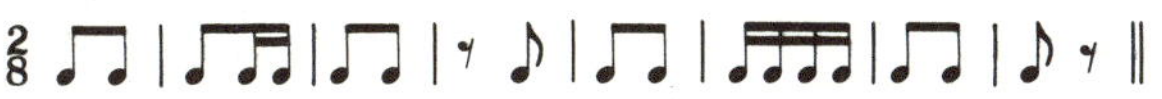

14. 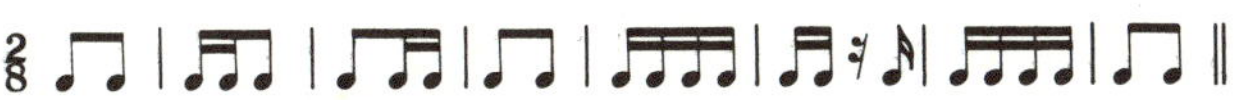

15. 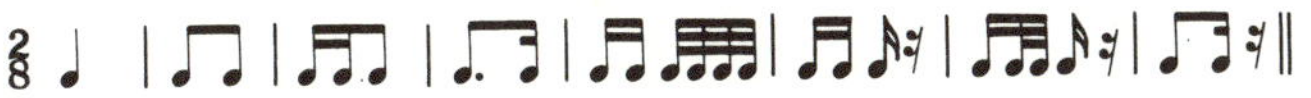

16. 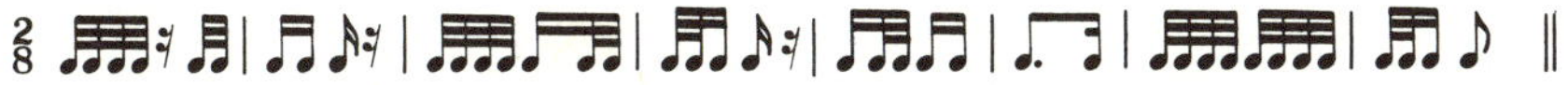

Simple Triple Meter, the "Three-Beat"

Measures in triple meter contain three beats: $\frac{3}{4}$, $\frac{3}{2}$, $\frac{3}{8}$, and $\frac{3}{16}$ (relatively rare). The most commonly used of these signatures is $\frac{3}{4}$; therefore most of our exercises are in that meter. However, you should also practice the other four time signatures carefully, so that you become accustomed to the visual aspects as well as the problems of the larger and smaller rhythmic values they contain.

Preparatory Exercises

Repeat each fragment several times, always conducting the "three" pattern until they are all completely mastered. Then proceed to the regular triple meter exercises. Once again, begin each fragment or exercise slowly (the basic unit = 60) and gradually increase the speed so that each can be performed eventually at a much greater speed (the basic unit = 100).

9. 

10. 

11. 

12. 

Regular Exercises

All exercises should be conducted while they are performed.

1. 

2. 

3. 

4. 

5. 

6. 

7. 

8. 

9. 

10. 

11. 

12. 3/2 [rhythmic notation]

13. 3/8 [rhythmic notation]

14. 3/8 [rhythmic notation]

15. 3/8 [rhythmic notation]

16. 3/8 [rhythmic notation]

17. 3/16 [rhythmic notation]

18. 3/16 [rhythmic notation]

19. 3/16 [rhythmic notation]

20. 3/16 [rhythmic notation]

Simple Quadruple Meter, the "Four-Beat"

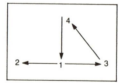

Measures in quadruple meter contain four beats: $\frac{4}{4}$, $\frac{4}{8}$, $\frac{4}{16}$, $\frac{4}{2}$. The most commonly used of these, $\frac{4}{4}$, will comprise the bulk of our exercises, including all of the preliminary fragments. However, $\frac{4}{8}$ and $\frac{4}{16}$ are quite common meter signatures today, while $\frac{4}{2}$ was a popular signature in the Renaissance and Baroque periods and is still used today. Therefore, as previously suggested, study them all carefully, in order to accustom yourself to the visual aspects of larger and smaller rhythmic values in each signature.

Preparatory Exercises

Follow the same directions as those given for the duple and triple meter exercises: repeat each preliminary fragment until mastered, and perform it (as well as the regular quadruple exercises) slowly at first (the basic unit = 60), eventually reaching a higher speed (the basic unit = 100).

SIMPLE (COMMON) METER

Regular Exercises

15. [musical notation]

16. [musical notation]

17. [musical notation]

18. [musical notation]

19. [musical notation]

20. [musical notation]

Syncopation

Syncopation, which literally means "cutting up," can be described as a situation in which the metric accent occurs on the normally weak beat instead of coinciding with the regular metric pattern. It may be called a displacement, and in these situations it is important to note that syncopation results when the pitches fail to fall *on the beat* with some *frequency* and *consistency*. Syncopation obscures the basic beat, and in some nineteenth- and twentieth-century pieces it even has a blurring effect on the rhythm. Syncopation can be accomplished by:

a. tying over the strong beat (which in $\frac{2}{4}$ and $\frac{3}{4}$ is the first beat and in $\frac{4}{4}$ the first and third beats of a measure):

[musical notation]

145

b. placing a rest on the strong beat:

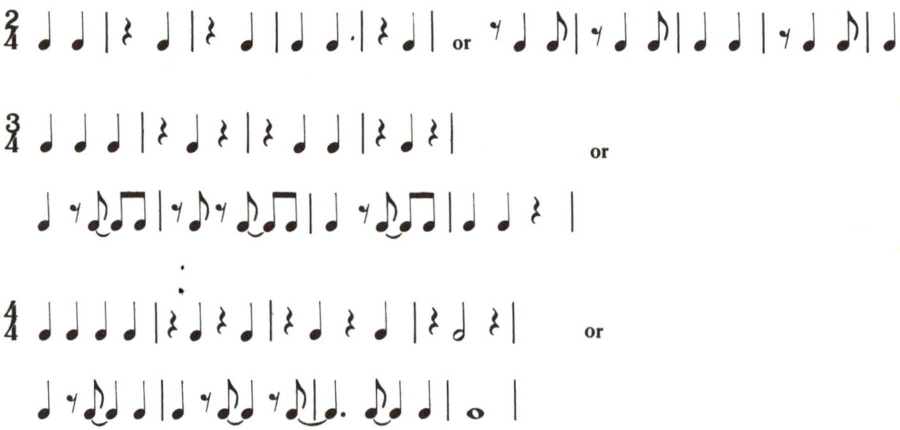

c. placing an accent on the weak beat:

The Anacrusis or Upbeat

Pieces or phrases may begin on beats other than the first beat of a measure. If this happens, it is customary to balance the incomplete measure at the beginning of the piece or phrase with a similarly incomplete measure at the end of that piece or phrase. The preliminary note or notes are called *anacrusis* or *upbeat(s)*.

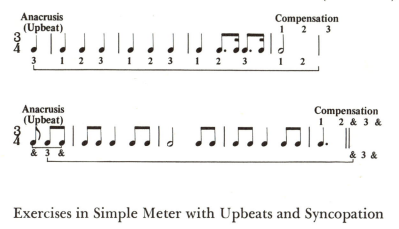

Exercises in Simple Meter with Upbeats and Syncopation

1. (music notation)

2. (music notation)

3. (music notation)

4. (music notation)

5. (music notation)

6. (music notation)

7. (music notation)

8. (music notation)

9. (music notation)

10. (music notation)

11. (music notation)

SIMPLE (COMMON) METER

Irregular Division of a Beat in Simple Meter

Up to this point, we have divided each beat into two or a multiple of two equal parts:

Each beat may be divided by other multiples, however, such as three, five, seven, nine, or more, in the following manner:

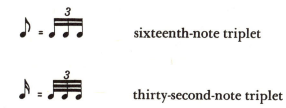

<table>
<tr><td>triplet</td></tr>
<tr><td>quarter-note triplet</td></tr>
<tr><td>half-note triplet</td></tr>
</table>

more infrequently:

sixteenth-note triplet

thirty-second-note triplet

In other words, each beat or unit above contains three equal subbeats or divisions. Below, a single beat or unit is divided into five subbeats or divisions:

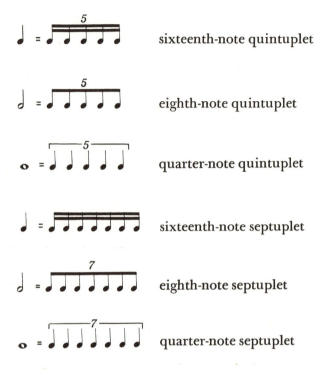

Above, a single beat or unit is divided into seven subbeats or divisions.

These are the most frequently encountered irregular divisions and should be practiced in the following exercises. Further irregular sub-divisions will be introduced in Chapter XIV.

Preparatory Exercises

Practice each fragment many times. In order to achieve clarity and evenness, say the numbers aloud which reflect the subdivisions. Do not conduct these exercises, but set a metronome and clap at about 50 for the basic unit. When a rest occurs in any irregular division of the beat, say the numbers for the sounded notes, and be silent for the rests:

SIMPLE (COMMON) METER

Regular Exercises

Practice each fragment many times until the subdivisions are absolutely even. The greater the subdivision of the beat, especially the septuplet, the slower the practice tempo should be. In these exercises, it may help to perform the triplets, quadruplets, and septuplets by saying the numbers themselves in order to assure greater evenness. All of these beat patterns must, of course, be conducted using the beat patterns pictured above.

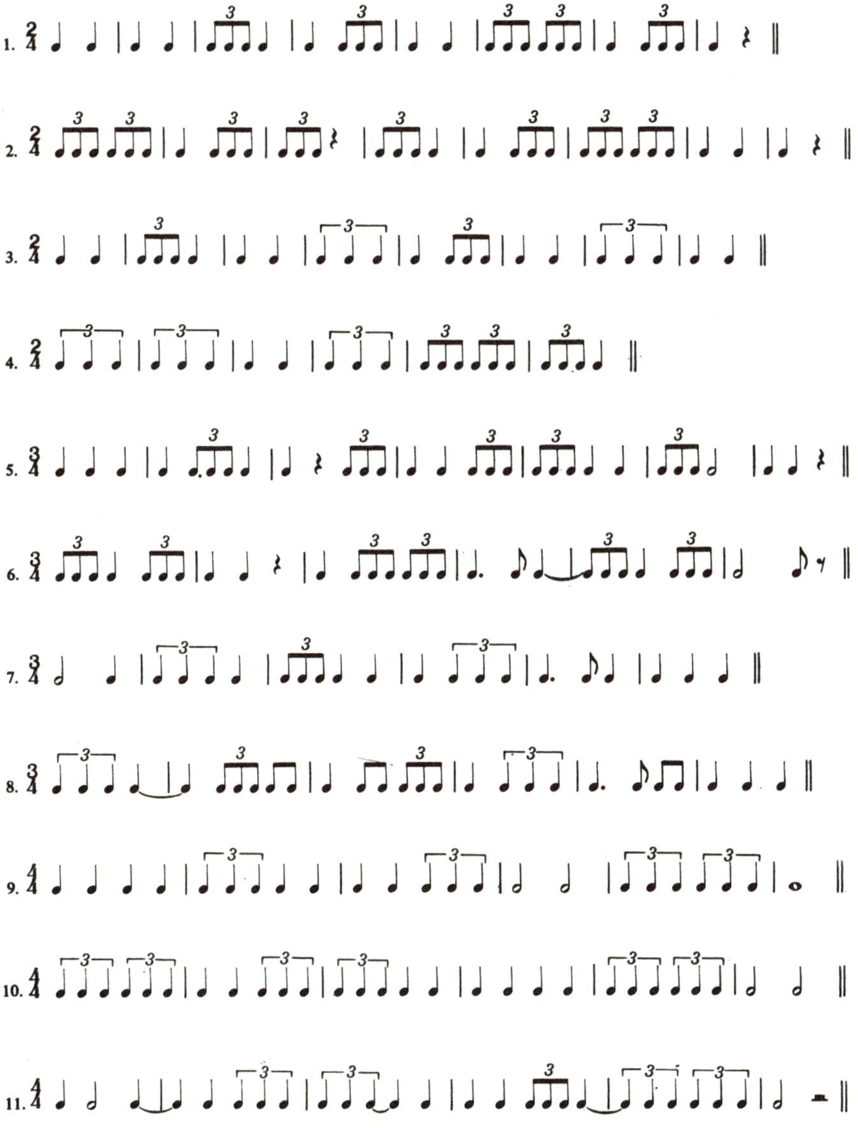

SIMPLE (COMMON) METER

154

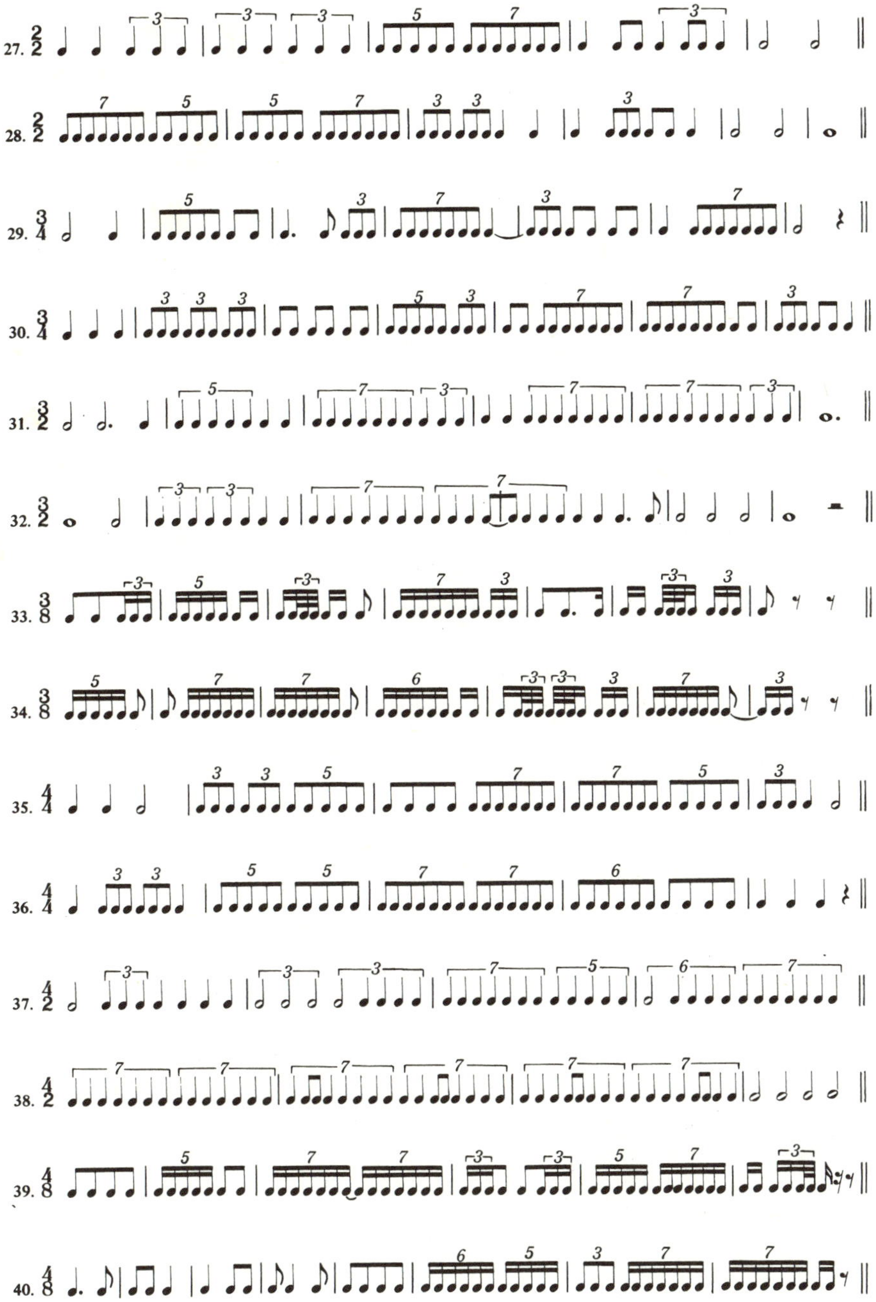
27.
28.
29.
30.
31.
32.
33.
34.
35.
36.
37.
38.
39.
40.

CHAPTER XII

Compound Meter

Meters that use triple rather than duple units are called *compound meters*. In other words, the upper numbers in simple-meter signatures are multiplied by three: thus, $\frac{2}{4}$ (simple) becomes $\frac{6}{8}$ (compound), $\frac{3}{4}$ (simple) becomes $\frac{9}{8}$ (compound), $\frac{4}{4}$ (simple) becomes $\frac{12}{8}$ (compound).

Both simple (common) and compound conducted in 2:

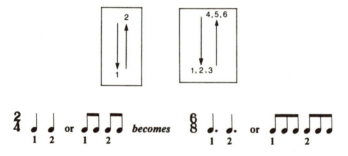

Both simple (common) and compound conducted in 3:

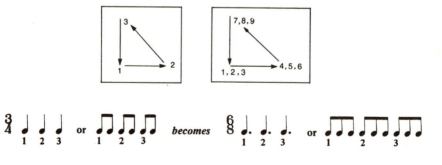

Both simple (common) and compound conducted in 4:

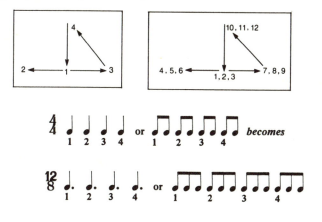

Similarly,

simple	compound	simple	compound	simple	compound
$\frac{2}{2}$ becomes $\frac{6}{4}$		$\frac{3}{2}$ becomes $\frac{9}{4}$		$\frac{4}{2}$ becomes $\frac{12}{4}$	
$\frac{2}{8}$ becomes $\frac{6}{16}$		$\frac{3}{8}$ becomes $\frac{9}{16}$		$\frac{4}{8}$ becomes $\frac{12}{16}$	

Compound Duple Meter ($\frac{6}{8}$, $\frac{6}{4}$, $\frac{6}{16}$)

Preparatory Exercises

Practice each fragment several times, always conducting the pattern while performing. Be sure that each accented beat contains three equal counts.

4. $\frac{6}{8}$ ♩. ♩. | ♫♩. | ♩. ♫ | ♩. ♩. | ♩. ‖

5. $\frac{6}{8}$ ♩. ♫ | ♫♩. | ♫♫ | ♩. ♩. ‖

6. $\frac{6}{8}$ ♫♫ | ♩. ♩. | ♩. ♫ | ♫♩. | ♩. ‖

7. $\frac{6}{8}$ ♩. ♩. | ♫♫ | ♩. ♩. | ♫♩. | ♩. ♫ ‖

8. $\frac{6}{8}$ ♩. | ♩. ♩. | ♩. ♫ | ♫♩. | ♫♫ ‖

9. $\frac{6}{8}$ ♩. ♩. | ♩ ♪♩. | ♫♩ ♪ | ♩. ♫ ‖

10. $\frac{6}{8}$ ♩. ♩ ♪ | ♪♩ ♩. | ♫♫ | ♩ ♪♩. ‖

11. $\frac{6}{8}$ ♪♩ ♩ ♪ | ♫♩. | ♫♩ ♪ | ♩. ♩. ‖

12. $\frac{6}{8}$ ♫♫ | ♫♩ ♪ | ♩. ♫ ♫ | ♫♪♩ ‖

Regular Exercises

Practice each exercise slowly at first (the basic unit = 50), increasing the speed gradually until each one can be performed at a fast, steady tempo (the basic unit = 100).

The following exercise employs *hemiola*, a technique involving time values in the relationship of 3:2. For instance, three half notes in the place of two dotted half notes:

$\frac{6}{4}$ ♩. ♩. | ♩ ♩ ♩   or $\frac{3}{4}$ ♩. | ♩. | ♩ ♩♩ ♩ |

This change from $\frac{6}{4}$ to $\frac{3}{4}$ and vice versa has frequently been used from the Baroque period through the present. Some notable examples may be found in Brahms, as in the opening of the *Third Symphony*.

COMPOUND METER

15.

16.

17.

18.

19.

Compound Triple Meter ($\frac{9}{8}$, $\frac{9}{4}$, $\frac{9}{16}$)

Preparatory Exercises

Practice each fragment several times, always conducting the pattern while performing. Be sure that each beat contains three *equal* counts.

1.

2.

3.

4.

5.

6.

7.

8. [music notation]

9. [music notation]

10. [music notation]

11. [music notation]

12. [music notation]

Regular Exercises

Practice each exercise slowly at first (the basic unit = 50), increasing the speed gradually until each one can be performed at a fast, steady tempo (the basic unit = 100).

1. [music notation]

2. [music notation]

3. [music notation]

4. [music notation]

5. [music notation]

6. [music notation]

7. [music notation]

8. [music notation]

9.

10.

11.

12.

13.

14.

15.

16.

17.

18.

Compound Quadruple Meter ($\frac{12}{8}$, $\frac{12}{4}$, $\frac{12}{16}$)

Preparatory Exercises

Practice each fragment several times, always conducting the patterns while performing. Be sure that each beat contains three equal counts.

1.

2.

Regular Exercises

Practice each exercise slowly at first (the basic unit = 50), increasing the speed gradually until each one can be performed at a fast, steady tempo (the basic unit = 100).

Additional Compound Meters

There are examples in music of all creative periods of works written with six, nine, or twelve beats in a measure. These are still notated in the same groupings as the compound meters encountered in the earlier part of this chapter, but they must be conducted in 6, 9, and 12. In order that you may become familiar with the different conducting patterns, as well as the feeling of compound meters that emphasize each beat rather than falling into patterns of 2, 3 and 4, do the following exercises carefully.

6/8, 6/4, 6/16

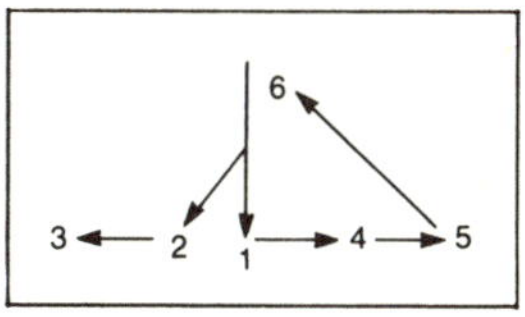

Practice each of the following slowly (the basic unit = 60), then increase speed gradually to about 100 for the basic unit, conducting each exercise with the "six" pattern printed above. Never get so fast that the beat is forced into a "two" pattern.

1. 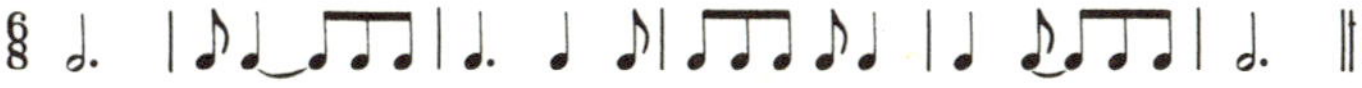

2. 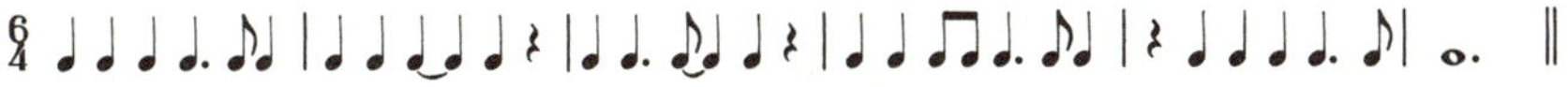

3. 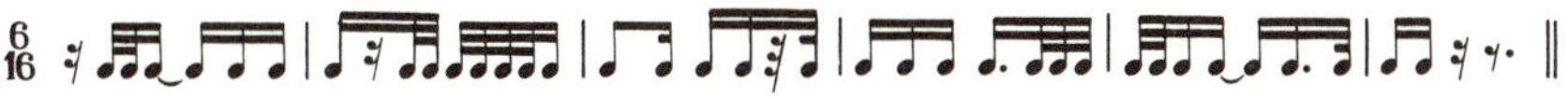

4. 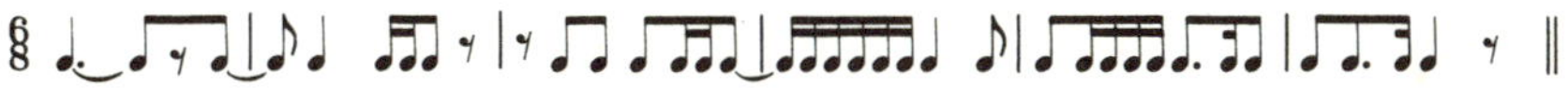

5. 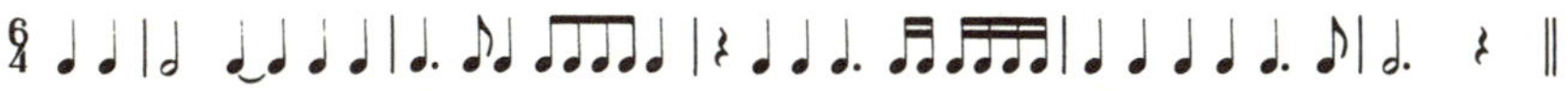

6. 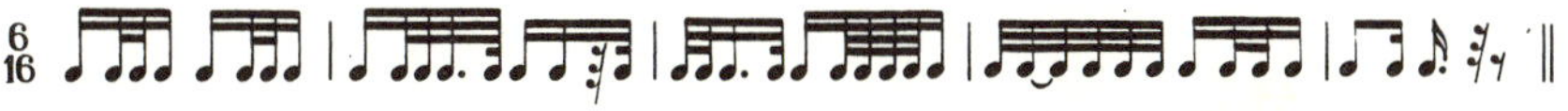

7. 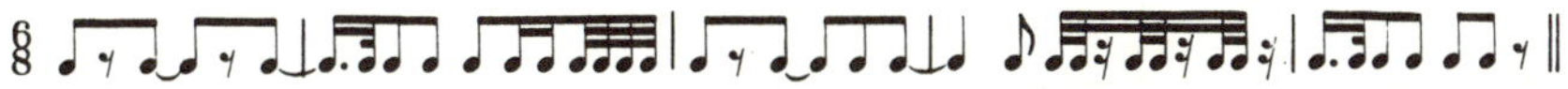

8. 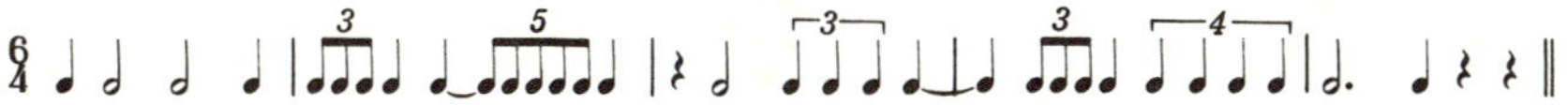

9. 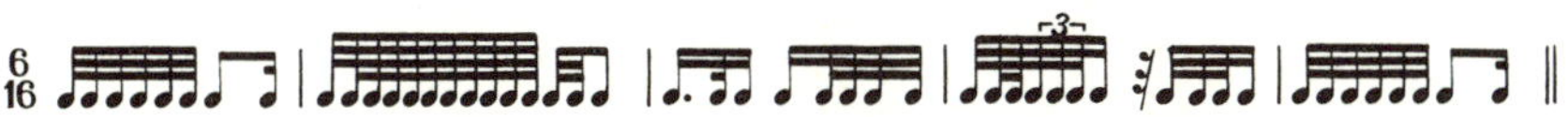

10. 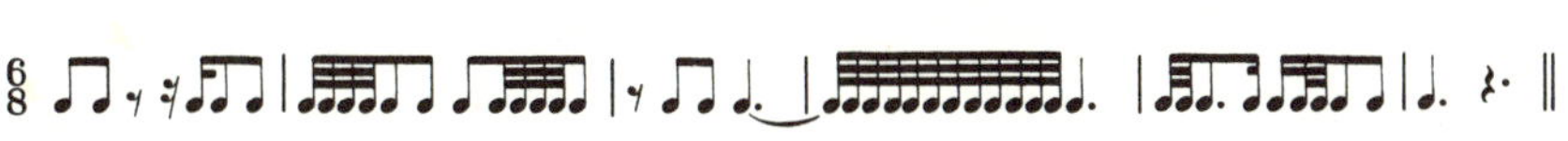

11. 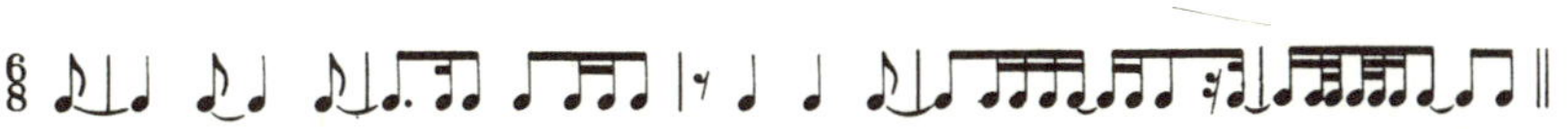

12. 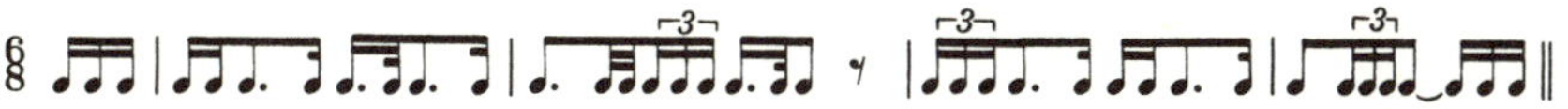

COMPOUND METER

For additional practice, use the regular exercises on pages 159-60 and perform (conduct) them in six rather than in two.

$$\frac{9}{8}, \frac{9}{16}, \frac{9}{4}$$

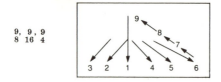

Practice each exercise slowly (the basic unit = 60), then increase speed gradually (to about 100 for the basic unit), conducting each exercise with the "nine" pattern printed above. Never get so fast that the beat is forced into a "three" pattern.

11.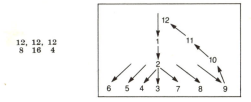

12.

For additional practice, use the regular exercises on pages 161-62 and perform (conduct) them in nine rather than in three.

12, 12, 12
8   16   4

Practice each exercise slowly (the basic unit = 60), then increase speed gradually (to about 100 for the basic unit), conducting each exercise with the "twelve" pattern printed above. Never get so fast that the beat is forced into a "four" pattern.

1.

2.

3.

4.

5.

6.

7.

COMPOUND METER

For additional practice, use the regular exercises on pages 163-64 and perform (conduct) them in twelve rather than in four.

CHAPTER XIII

Composite Meters

All meters practiced thus far, both simple and compound, have a certain amount of symmetry within a given measure. Each beat within a measure has been of equal duration. In the composite or complex compound meters, one or more beats within a measure are elongated.

Quintuple Meter: $\frac{5}{8}$, $\frac{5}{16}$, $\frac{5}{4}$

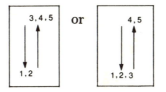

Five-eight is made up of two plus three eighth notes (for eighth notes, substitute sixteenths or quarters in $\frac{5}{16}$ or $\frac{5}{4}$) and is conducted in two, with one short and one elongated beat to each measure. Usually the composer indicates what division of the measure he desires, whether $2 + 3$ or $3 + 2$. Special attention must be paid to assuring that all eighth, quarter, or sixteenth notes within a measure of composite meter are absolutely equal, so that $\frac{5}{8}$ ♪♩♫ does not sound like ♪♩♫ .

COMPOSITE METERS

Preparatory Exercises

Perform these fragments slowly and carefully, conducting each one as it is executed. Repeat each one until it feels natural before you proceed to the regular exercises. It will be helpful at first if you accent the first note in each group slightly when you practice these exercises.

Regular Exercises

Practice each exercise slowly, beginning at 100 for the basic unit. Then increase the speed gradually until it reaches about 156 for the basic unit. Be certain that all units, whether quarter, eighth, or sixteenth, remain equal throughout each exercise.

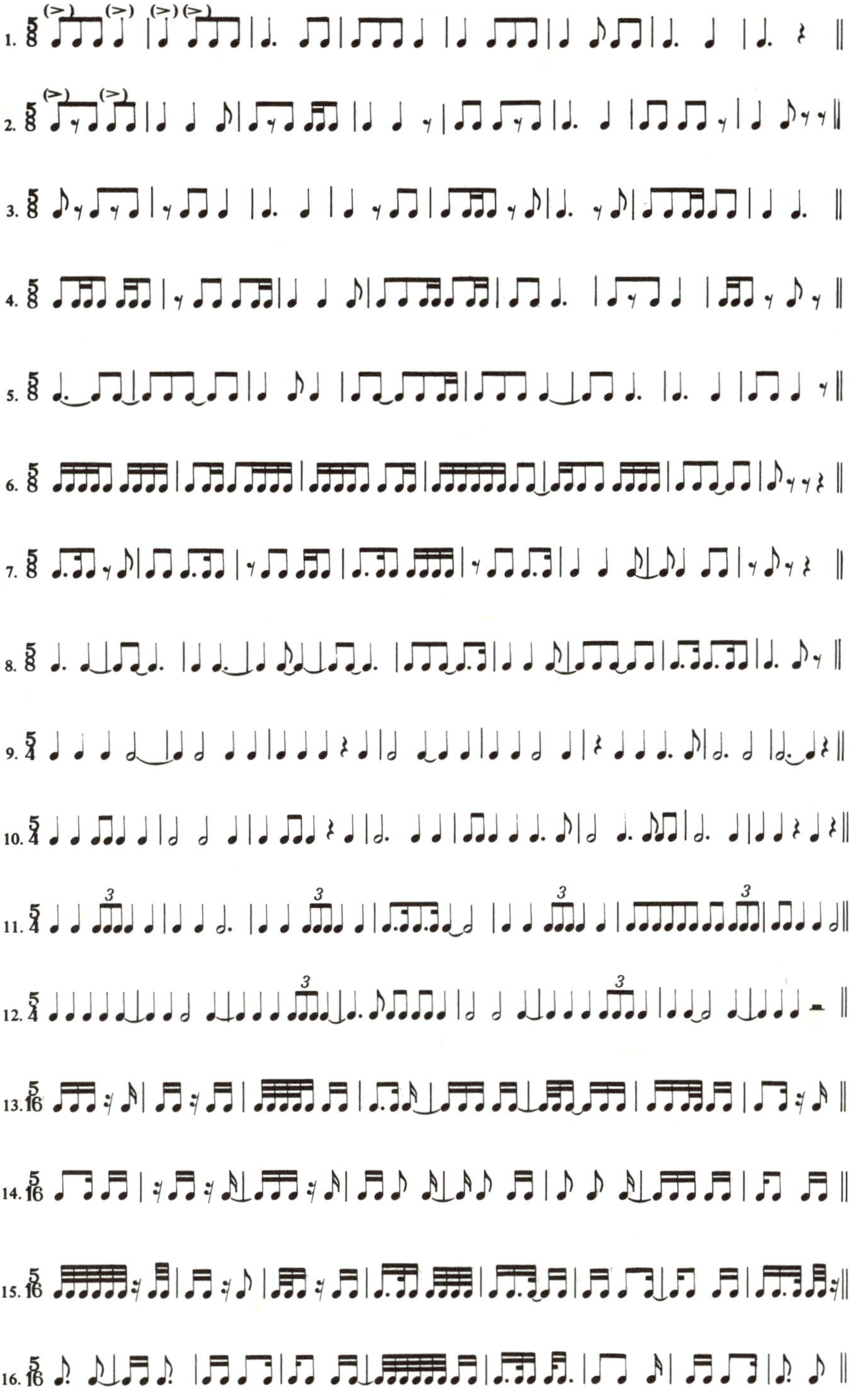
1. 5 8
2. 5 8
3. 5 8
4. 5 8
5. 5 8
6. 5 8
7. 5 8
8. 5 8
9. 5 4
10. 5 4
11. 5 4
12. 5 4
13. 5 16
14. 5 16
15. 5 16
16. 5 16

COMPOSITE METERS

Septuple Meter: $\frac{7}{8}$, $\frac{7}{16}$, $\frac{7}{4}$

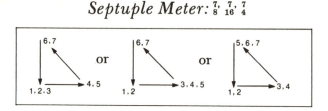

Seven-eight is made up of two plus two plus three eighth notes (substitute sixteenths or quarters for eighths in $\frac{7}{16}$ or $\frac{7}{4}$) and is conducted in three, with two equal and one elongated beat. Three combinations are usual: $2 + 2 + 3$, $3 + 2 + 2$, and $2 + 3 + 2$. Once again, pay close attention to the length of the beats, so that the durations of all sixteenths, eighths, or quarters are absolutely equal throughout each exercise.

Preparatory Exercises

Perform these fragments slowly and carefully, conducting each as it is executed. Repeat each one until it feels comfortable before you proceed to the regular exercises.

Regular Exercises

Practice each one slowly, beginning at 100 for the basic unit. Then increase the speed gradually until you reach about 156 for the basic unit. Be certain that all units, whether quarters, eighths, or sixteenths, remain equal throughout each exercise.

14. 7/16 [musical notation]

15. 7/16 [musical notation]

16. 7/16 [musical notation]

Conduct all the regular quintuple and septuple meter exercises in slow motion, that is in the slow five and slow seven pattern. You will find these composite or complex compound rhythms used in both slow and fast tempos, so it is important to master the composite patterns (in 2 and 3) as well as the complex compound patterns (in 5 and 7).

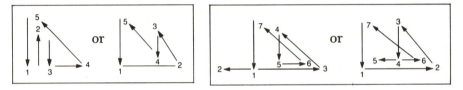

Division of Compound Meters into Irregular Patterns

As we have already seen in the case of 6/8 or 6/4 meter, composers often divide measures into somewhat irregular patterns in order to create new accentuations within an established rhythm. The classical, most familiar example of this practice is the *hemiola* (discussed on page 158):

6/8 [notation] is often divided 6/8 [notation] (actually 3/4);

6/4 [notation] is often divided 6/4 [notation] (actually 3/2).

The 9/8 or 9/4 measure may appear in several configurations, and usually the composer specifies how it is to be "felt" and conducted if it deviates from the norm. He may place accents at certain points, or bar the eighth notes, or put "in 4" at the beginning of the phrase. Conducting will become a bit more complex in these situations, since one of the beats must be elongated. Here is the way it is usually done:

Conducted in 4

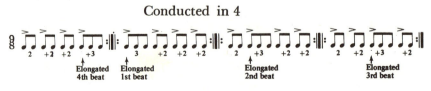

Practice each of the patterns above separately, until each one feels natural. Then go on to the following exercises which feature $\frac{6}{8}$, $\frac{6}{4}$, $\frac{9}{8}$, and $\frac{9}{4}$ meters in regular and irregular accentuations within the measure.

Additional Composite Meters

Other composite meters with elongated beats may be encountered in configurations of measures in $\frac{8,\ 8,\ 8}{8\ \ 4\ \ 16}$; $\frac{10,\ 10,\ 10}{8\ \ \ 4\ \ \ 16}$; and $\frac{11,\ 11,\ 11}{8\ \ \ 4\ \ \ 16}$. Practice the given patterns carefully, then do the exercises using these rhythmic patterns, always keeping the quarter, eighth, and sixteenth values equal.

Basic Patterns

a. $\frac{8,\ 8,\ 8}{8\ \ 4\ \ 16}$, conducted in 3

b. $\frac{10}{8}$, conducted in 4

c. $\frac{11}{8}$, conducted in 4

Exercises

Conduct $\frac{8}{8}$, $\frac{10}{8}$, $\frac{11}{8}$ in either 3 or 4, with elongated beats. Some of these will alternate between $\frac{4}{4}$ and $\frac{8}{8}$, $\frac{4}{4}$ and $\frac{10}{8}$, $\frac{4}{4}$ and $\frac{11}{8}$.

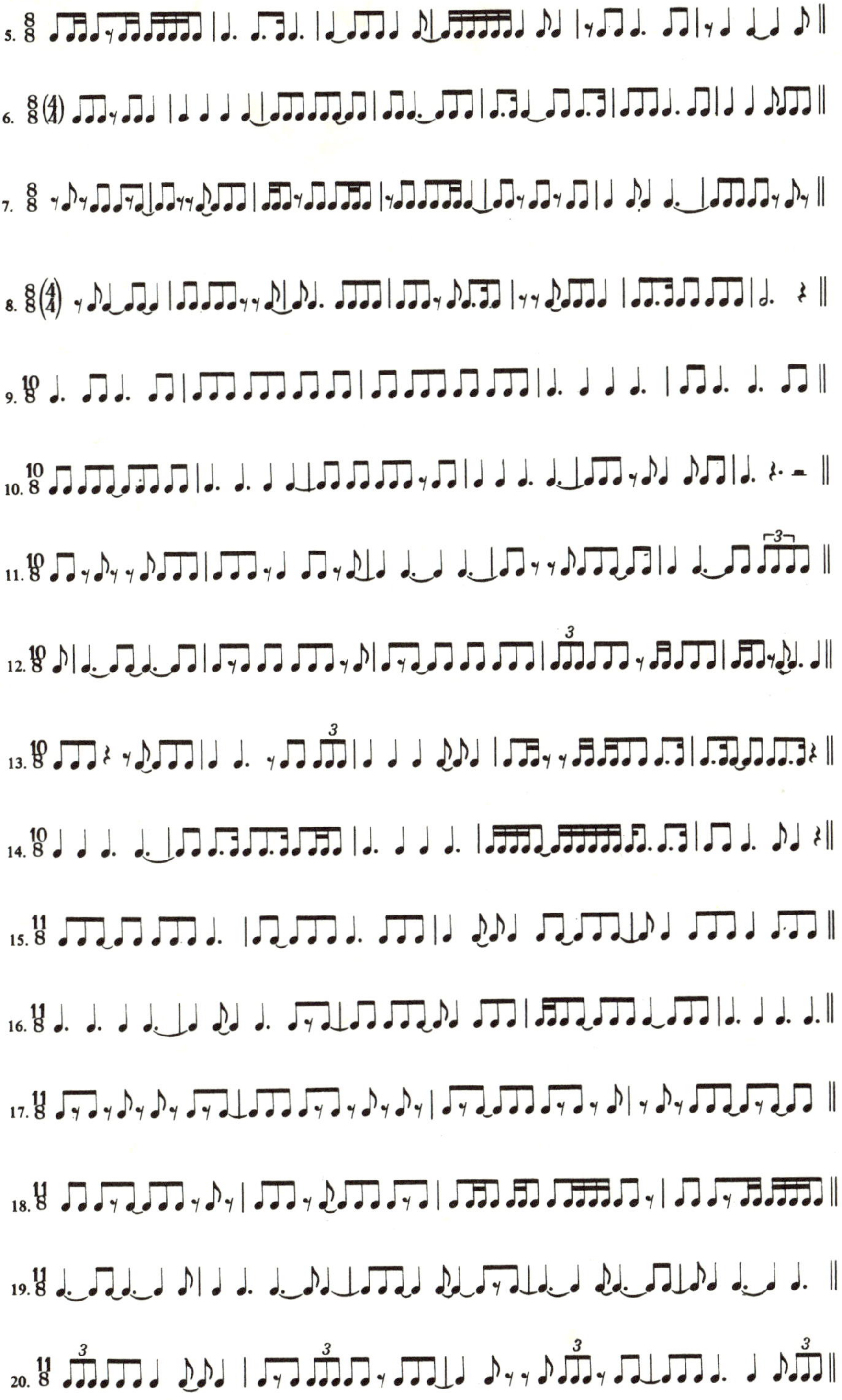
5. 8/8
6. 8/8 (4/4)
7. 8/8
8. 8/8 (4/4)
9. 10/8
10. 10/8
11. 10/8
12. 10/8
13. 10/8
14. 10/8
15. 11/8
16. 11/8
17. 11/8
18. 11/8
19. 11/8
20. 11/8

COMPOSITE METERS

There are occasions when $\frac{8}{16}$, $\frac{10}{16}$, and $\frac{11}{16}$ time signatures will occur. Therefore, practice these exercises to accustom yourself to the smaller note values. Conduct in 3 or 4, as above.

CHAPTER XIV

Further Rhythmic Devices

Mixed (Changing) Meters

In previous chapters, we have seen how composers have tried to free themselves from the "tyranny of the barline" by such means as syncopation, shifting accentuation, hemiola, and others. With the exception of isolated famous examples, it was not until the end of the nineteenth century and the beginning of the twentieth that mixed or changing meters were used extensively. The popularity of folk, jazz, and rhythmic speech elements and their use in concert music have contributed to the frequent use of these devices in the twentieth century. Usually, unless otherwise specified, the basic unit remains constant, even though the number of units in each measure changes. In the sequence of measures marked $\frac{2}{4}\frac{3}{4}\frac{5}{4}\frac{6}{4}\frac{4}{4}$, the quarter note remains constant in each measure, while in the sequence $\frac{4}{8}\frac{9}{8}\frac{3}{8}\frac{5}{8}\frac{7}{8}\frac{2}{8}$, the eighth note is the constant factor. When measures of eighth-note units are mixed with higher-value units, it is best to feel the smallest unit as the constant factor, so that in the sequence $\frac{4}{4}\frac{5}{8}\frac{7}{8}\frac{3}{4}\frac{2}{4}\frac{6}{8}$, it is suggested that the eighth note be established as the common unit.

Regular Exercises

Practice each exercise slowly, conducting while performing. Then try to increase speed, never reaching a tempo that would make the smallest units seem rushed. Be certain throughout these exercises that the eighth note remains constant.

RHYTHMIC DEVICES

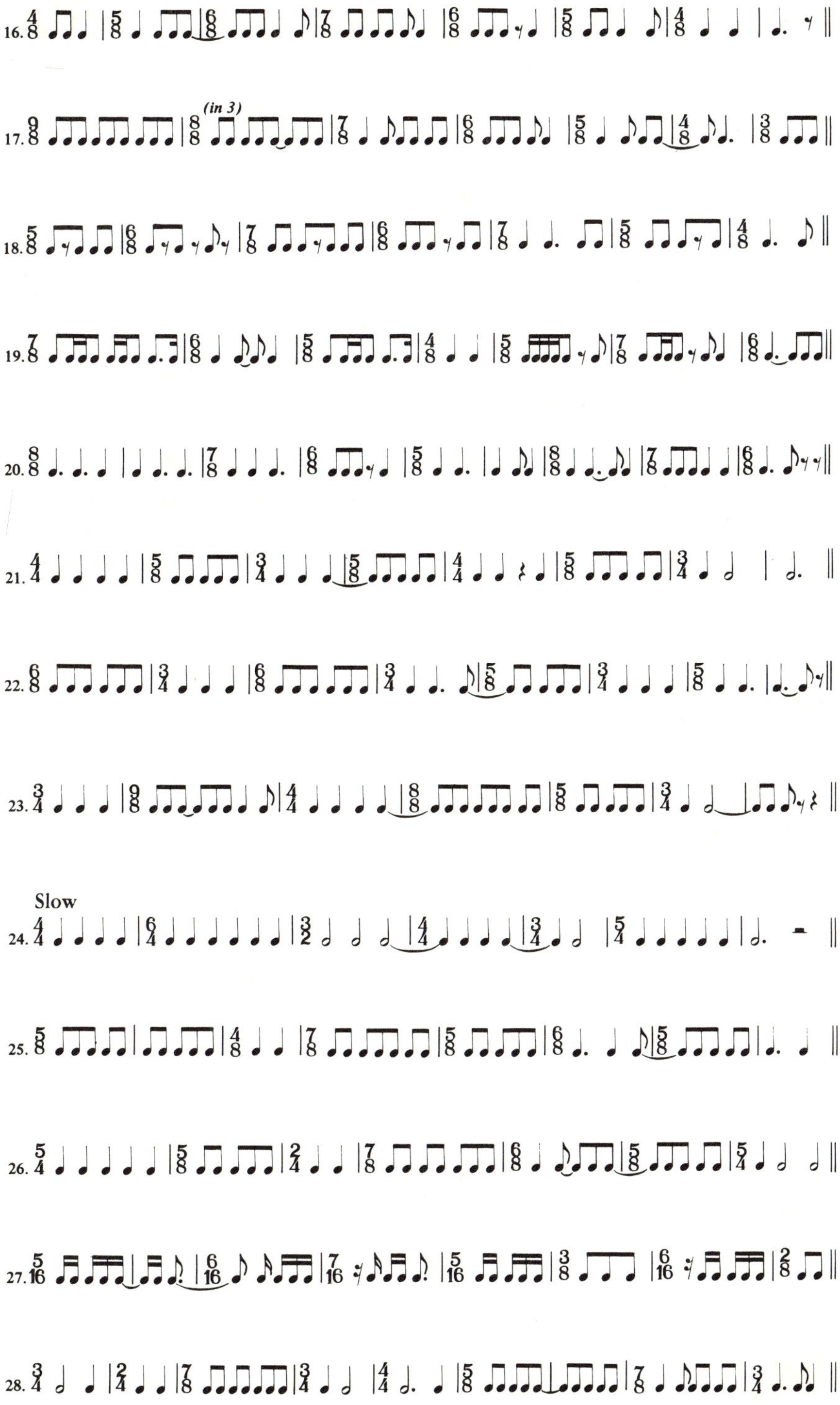
16.
(in 3)
17.
18.
19.
20.
21.
22.
23.
Slow
24.
25.
26.
27.
28.

Complex Divisions of the Beat

We have, thus far, divided the individual beats into triplets, quadruplets, quintuplets, sextuplets, septuplets, and others. The next step is to practice situations where a different number of notes replaces the normal amount of notes over a predetermined time span.

Examples

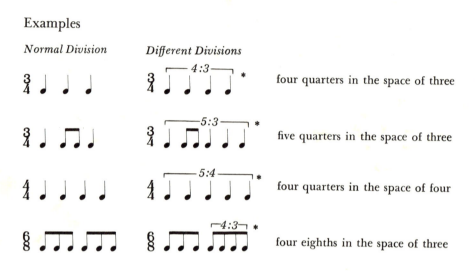

Normal Division   *Different Divisions*

four quarters in the space of three

five quarters in the space of three

four quarters in the space of four

four eighths in the space of three

These examples abound, especially in twentieth-century music. Practice the exercises slowly and carefully, once again giving special attention to evenness in all the complex divisions of the beat or beats.

Exercises

* Sometimes the designation is simply ⌐‾‾‾⌐ or ⌐‾‾‾⌐. It is less specific, but still signifies the same idea—that of having four or five notes in the space of the normal number of notes.

Thirty-Four Duets

The top line of these duets should be "sung" or "spoken" on a convenient syllable similar to those used in previous chapters (*la, ta, doo, loo, da,* etc.). The bottom part should be tapped or clapped. These duets may be performed by two people or two parts of a class, but they should also be practiced and performed by a single individual doing both parts simultaneously.

183

RHYTHMIC DEVICES